The Spiritual Genius of Thomas Merton

The Spiritual Genius of Thomas Merton

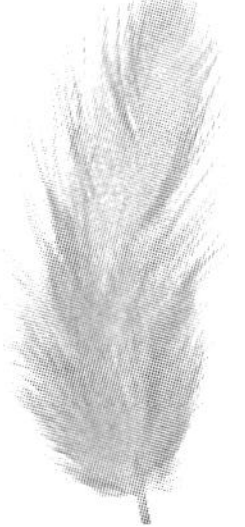

Anthony T. Padovano

Franciscan Media
Cincinnati, Ohio

Portions of this book were previously published as *The Human Journey: Thomas Merton, Symbol of a Century* (New York: Doubleday, 1982).Scripture passages have been taken from *New Revised Standard Version Bible,* copyright ©1989 by the Division of Christian Education of the National Council of the Churches of Christ in the U.S.A., and used by permission. All rights reserved.

Cover and book design by Mark Sullivan
Cover image © PhotoXpress | milosluz

Library of Congress Cataloging-in-Publication Data
Padovano, Anthony T.
[Human journey]
The spiritual genius of Thomas Merton / Anthony T. Padovano.
pages cm
Rev. ed. of: The human journey : Thomas Merton, symbol of a century. 1982.
Includes bibliographical references.
ISBN 978-1-61636-802-9 (alk. paper)
1. Merton, Thomas, 1915-1968. 2. Trappists—United States—Biography. I. Title.
BX4705.M542P33 2014
271'.12502—dc23
2014030234

ISBN 978-1-61636-802-9

Published by Franciscan Media
28 W. Liberty St.
Cincinnati, OH 45202
www.FranciscanMedia.org

Printed in the United States of America.
Printed on acid-free paper.
14 15 16 17 18 5 4 3 2 1

For

•

Theresa

Mark Anthony

Andrew Anthony

Paul Anthony

Rosemarie Theresa

•

CONTENTS

FOREWORD

A Genius for Reconciling the Irreconcilable

January 31, 2015, is the one-hundredth anniversary of Thomas Merton's birth. The International Thomas Merton Society will honor his centenary at Bellarmine University's Thomas Merton Center in Louisville, Kentucky, home to the largest archive of his legacy. Other libraries across the United States, possessing significant collections of his work, will host special exhibitions. Articles noting his continuing prominence will appear in a range of periodicals. Lectures and retreats will be held in other countries, since his books are still in print in over fifteen languages. If you are wondering why all the fuss, Anthony T. Padovano can mentor your appreciation of Merton's currency for our lives today, forty-six years after the monk's death in Bangkok, Thailand in 1968.

The Spiritual Genius of Thomas Merton is a finely crafted survey of the dynamic spirits that moved through Merton's life and works. Padovano exhibits an unusual empathy with the inner meaning of the monk's literary career. As a professor of literature, he situates Merton's place in the stream of American cultural history. As a skilled writer himself, he juxtaposes and blends early and late moments in Merton's biography that reveal unsuspected continuities in his often conflicted self-expressions. As a theologian, he examines the parameters of the monk's soul as he struggles for personal integration while seeking God. Like a field archeologist, he excavates below the surface of Merton's lively and enthusiastic personality to find the solid foundations that supported the always expansive character of his dialogues with the world.

This text is a new edition of Padovano's *The Human Journey: Thomas Merton, Symbol of a Century*, republished and updated in response to requests that he review his seminal work and make it accessible to another generation of readers. When it was first published in 1982, Padovano's book moved me deeply so that I requested an interview with him for publication in *The Merton Annual*. In this portion of the interview, he discusses the central theme of this book:

Montaldo: I want to preface my questions on *The Human Journey* by remarking that, as time passes and when all of Thomas Merton's primary material is published or accessible, it's my assessment that *The Human Journey* will remain an important and decisively perceptive study on Merton's life and influence. Your prose and your analysis resonate deeply with symbols and metaphors embedded in Merton's writing. Were Merton alive today to read the secondary literature published since his death, I think he would enjoy and learn from *The Human Journey*. Rehearse for me the reasons for your calling Thomas Merton a "symbol for a century."

Padovano: My concern was to figure out why this man has the appeal that he does. What is there in this man that is so attractive? Merton's appeal did not originate with any one element in his writing that in itself was so extraordinary it merited world-class attention. So as I went through the elements I kept saying, "Well, where's the appeal?" And the appeal seemed to be in two things: first, in the fusion of biography and theology. Secondly, and perhaps more important, Merton resonates in a subliminal way for people when they read him; he captures the dynamics of the age in which they are living. He is dealing with the same tensions, the same problems, the same prospects that his readers are, but he is solving his difficulties by holding in tension what seem to be polarities. He deals with polarities such as the sacred and the secular, East and West, male and female, conscience and authority;, polarities that fuse brilliantly in his writing....

In the nineteenth century, for example, the either/or mentality prevailed. One was either this or that. In the twentieth century we are trying to say that, ""No, maybe we are both/and. We are both Catholic and Protestant, both male and female, both East and West."" In the twentieth century the preference is toward balance. What would have been seen in the nineteenth century as a betrayal of principle—one had to be totally one thing to the exclusion of anything else, one true Church and all the others were false—in the twentieth century is seen as intellectually myopic and emotionally arrogant.

Montaldo: You said that Merton seemed to solve the problem of "dialectics," which is your technical word for the tensions inherent between two apparently irreconcilable experiences or ideas. But I would not say that Merton "solved" anything for himself or us, since, at least in my reading, Merton's personal tensions appear without solution. You yourself have said elsewhere that tensions exist in every aspect of our lives and that we not only cannot escape these tensions but we do not even have a right to escape them. Does Merton's writing really represent a solution to the "dialectics" of the twentieth century?

Padovano: In Merton there is what I might call an existential solution: his willingness to live with the tensions and to realize they can never be solved. Merton lived fully with the tensions inherent in ideas like conscience and authority, being unable and unwilling, I think on the deepest levels, to compromise an understanding of either conscience or authority in ways that would remove the inherent tension between them.

The non-resolution—if this is not playing with words too much—the non-resolution *is* a resolution in the sense that you realize this is the creative, healthy tension that you must live with for your whole life. So, I would say that Merton "solved" the tension by saying that the ambiguity is inescapable.

Anthony Padovano possesses a mind as wide-ranging as Merton's literary corpus. He presents a satisfyingly complex vision of Merton's message and its meaning. Reading this new edition of his valuable work has reassured me that my admiration for his achievement has held steady over decades and will endure.

—Jonathan Montaldo, archivist emeritus of the
Thomas Merton International Center

PREFACE

There are people in every era who manage somehow to represent its character. It is not always the uniqueness of their thought or the singularity of their accomplishments that does this. They become symbols because they feel and personalize the forces of an age more deeply and comprehensively than others. Thomas Merton is such a man.

The century in which Merton lived addressed tensions that previous centuries found contradictory but which had enormous creative possibilities in them. The character of the century was often tentative because certitude was challenged dramatically and often. This occurred in physics with Einstein's relativity and Heisenberg's principle of indeterminacy; in philosophy with theories of process, existentialism, and linguistic analysis; in theology with ecumenism, ecclesial reform, and biblical criticism.

Thomas Merton explored in his own life the convergence of authority and conscience, of sacred commitments and secular options, of Western ideas and Eastern beliefs, of medieval lifestyles and modern forms of social protest. The range of his thought and experience, the number of books and articles he wrote, the astounding variety of people he reached make him an intriguing and catholic thinker. The journey of his life appeared at all its stages as an unfinished and unsettled endeavor. He was always unpredictable.

This book will sketch the life of Merton in its elusiveness and assertiveness. The following chapters will deal with his faith and his writing, his poetry and conflicts, his mysticism and secularity, the psychological pressures that shaped his life and the myths that influenced his century.

Thomas Merton's ultimate appeal has something to do with his capacity to become part of us. His life is a preface to our own, a prelude to further possibilities and new directions.

PRELUDE

It was only New York. The East had not happened yet. It was still dark. But soon, soon in the light he would die. Just in time.

Strange. A Cistercian monk of the Strict Observance in New York to visit a Zen Buddhist scholar, D.T. Suzuki.

He was young when he was last in New York. Columbia University. Harlem.

Twenty-two years since he had been here. Drunk on the floor of Nick's Bar in Greenwich Village, murmuring repeatedly, "I'm going to be a priest! I'm going to be a priest!" Jinny was part of his life then, A Cistercian monk of the Strict Observance. A hermit, for God's sake. Sitting on the floor in his pajamas, drinking sherry on the rocks, listening to New York. Jinny Burton.

It all came together now. New York, as secular a city as cities can get. Here, of all places, a contemplative Catholic hermit is ready to meet a Zen Buddhist scholar. A Trappist monk—as Catholic and celibate as you can get. Wondering why he never married, regretting all that was lost along the way.

He was wild as an undergraduate at Columbia—he was at Columbia now, Butler Hall. He was worse at Cambridge. The sounds of New York. He was faithful to them. Twenty-two years of the strictest discipline the Catholic Church sanctions. And still not settled. Happy. Content. It does not last. Home. He had found the only home he had ever known. Now he was restless again. It was not enough. It never is enough.

The sherry was good. And New York, the love affair with New York was on again. He hated it once—but that was only because love frightened him.

The Nazis bombed Warsaw the last time he had seen her. The war had begun. Before it was over, Hiroshima would be incinerated. His mother's body was reduced to ashes.

Harlem always troubled him. He listened to it now. In an early poem he had seen America crucify Christ and children in Harlem. Sounds of anguish.

His journey was nearly over, but he did not know it then. He felt as though he had walked through the whole century. He would die before the century ended. But they belonged to each other—this century and Thomas Merton. All the Jinny Burtons, all the Harlems, all the prayers in the night, all the belongings. New York. Kentucky. Rome. Paris. London.

He became a symbol of the twentieth century—of its turmoil and sensitivity, of its conflict and restlessness, of its furtive peace and fugitive wars, of its holocausts and Hiroshimas and Harlems and hopes. Everyone he loved would die in this century. He would die too…soon. But death would not have an easy time of it.

CHAPTER ONE

A Wilderness Faith

Unusual dreams disturbed him. There were recurring dreams of women he could not reach. Sometimes they were black and emerged as his mother. On other occasions they had biblical names and eluded him. He dreamed he was a child in France and then a Buddhist monk. The beginning and the end. He is born in France; he dies in Bangkok.

And then there were, well, visions. His deceased father "appeared" to the young Hamlet struggling with his destiny and his conscience. There were moments of ecstasy. In Cuba, during the liturgy, he was overpowered with a sense of God. He became a Trappist soon after. At a busy corner in Louisville, he was seized by a new vocation and an awareness of solidarity with the entire human race. He became a social critic and a secular poet not much later.

It was not for these reasons that Thomas Merton was considered a mystic. The dreams and visions, the ecstasies and reveries, defined his pilgrimage rather than his mysticism. He was born to wander, like the century in which his life began and ended. Despite a commitment to monastic stability, he was as restless as America, as uprooted as the era in which he lived. His dreams were about the lands and the people he had missed along the way but refused to relinquish.

He was not an easy man to live with, nor a congenial thinker to rely on. He shifted gears emotionally and intellectually with rapidity, indeed an awkwardness that disturbed his readers as much as it unsettled the riders who became daring passengers in the trucks he drove. He was all tumult and tranquility. In his words one could catch the heartbreak and holiness of a century that wept with good reason and rejoiced in an unconventional manner.

Sanctity assumed an unexpected character in the century in which he lived and the country where he settled. Somehow Merton was part of both. The measure of his achievement could not be taken, as it often is in these matters, by times other than our own or by cultures that had little appreciation of the American influence.

He was a most unusual monk, an intense admixture of contradiction and contemplation, of wild secularity and antiquated piety, of savage protest and almost ingratiating sympathy. He wanted to be like many of the things he condemned. He abhorred and embraced New York. He supported and undercut radical reform. He renounced marriage and regretted the surrender.

The story of Thomas Merton holds our attention because we hear in its narrative the echoes and resonance of our personal histories. The journey of his life was arduous. The tentative steps led to little certitude. Publicly, he admitted he was sad and sick of himself. Privately, he confessed to a sense of nausea about his work and his frenetic, compulsive addiction to writing. The writing was a preservative against alcohol and seduction, a way of touching people without jeopardy to his celibacy and his contemplative calling.

"And I heard a voice saying, there is another side to the mountain."[1] This thought, which rings like a refrain in his last book, *The Asian Journal,* is a leitmotif for his life. There was always another side of the mountain. The only mountain that conquered him was the one that had no more faces, no new sides, no further summits.

A short time before his death, Merton was transfixed by the mountains of Asia, hypnotized and subdued by the inaccessibility and infinite alternatives offered by the topography of Asia for the geography of life. He was born again in Asia, a birth not in water or Spirit but in fire and death. He named his famous autobiography *The Seven Storey Mountain.* The mountain then was symbolic and the purgation required to scale it was internal, a break with friends and comfort, a severance from self-indulgence and self-affirmation. Now, in Asia, the mountains were physical and the price demanded of him was bodily pain. He died in the East, where the sun rises and the great religions of the world begin. He died alone and in silence, like the Zen Buddhism he admired and the eremitical life he cherished.

Thomas Merton's story is important for the insight it gives into the journey motif of his writing career. In isolation from his biography, Merton's thought sometimes seems unimpressive. His appeal lies in a fusion of life and thought that makes him captivating for the century he assimilates and challenges.

The story of Thomas Merton is worth preserving for the same reason that any good story is worth keeping. It enables us to get on in life, to see connections beyond the random happenings of everyday experience, and, most important, to participate in the process by which life is continuous. Narrative helps us appreciate how meaning emerges from the apparently patternless series of events we encounter.

Merton and American Culture

The experience of journey, geographic and metaphoric, has been a decisive element in the construction of American culture. The long voyage across the Atlantic and the arduous trek westward across the continent have shaped American consciousness indelibly. American literature is a remarkably accurate indicator of this national preoccupation.

From William Bradford's *History of Plymouth Plantation* through Mark Twain's *Adventures of Huckleberry Finn* and Herman Melville's *Moby Dick* to Hart Crane's *The Bridge* and John Steinbeck's *The Grapes of Wrath,* America has been transfixed by the idea of journey. Journey is not only an archetypal national quest. It is often a personal odyssey. For that reason, autobiography has been perhaps the form of writing most congenial to the American temper. Benjamin Franklin and Ralph Waldo Emerson, Henry David Thoreau and Henry Adams, Thomas Wolfe and Norman Mailer, Emily Dickinson and Walt Whitman are evidence of America's fascination with the self and more particularly with the self in search of an identity it never quite achieves.

Thomas Merton's work is more easily unified under the category of journey than under any other category. The journey is developed autobiographically from *The Seven Storey Mountain,* his first major work, to *The Asian Journal,* his last writing. Merton's appeal for Americans is premised on the narrative character of his work organized under the symbols of journey and the self.

It is possible to take our observation a step further, a step that brings us more deeply into the meaning of America and the mystery of Thomas Merton. It is not journey nor autobiography in general that is at the essence of American culture but, more specifically, spiritual autobiography. The belief that all people possess divinity within themselves supported the development of democratic political ideas in America.

The search for that divinity led to Puritan journals and diaries. It continued even into post-Puritan America in such secular accounts as Benjamin Franklin's *Autobiography.* The idea of analysis or at least mental record keeping as a way of discovering one's spiritual depths is very much alive in America today. The spiritual search is not always religious. It continues in its secular forms as an effort to define an aspect of the self that is endowed with integrity or excellence.

American literature has been fascinated with a homiletic, or sermon, style from the beginning. Puritans write sermons about Providence for their Sunday service. Ralph Waldo Emerson's inspirational essays are really secular sermons. Henry David Thoreau cajoles and thunders as he tries to awaken the world from its spiritual slumber and sloth. The sermon in *Moby Dick* and the wrestling by Ishmael with biblical texts continue the tradition.

Arthur Dimmesdale in *The Scarlet Letter* brings that classic to its completion by his sermon-confession. Henry Adams writes of virginity and dynamos as he summons America to a new vision in the early years of the twentieth century. The Easter sermon in William Faulkner's masterpiece, *The Sound and the Fury,* expresses the inner meaning of the story. The Declaration of Independence, the Gettysburg Address, Abraham Lincoln's Second Inaugural Address, Martin Luther King's "I Have a Dream" speech are political sermons as well as spiritual testimonies.

The Seven Storey Mountain is an effective and forceful presentation of this genre. Though contemporary America was not aware of it, spiritual autobiography was part of its heritage. There are needs in the American psyche that personal confession and spiritual autobiography have addressed from the beginning. They are now dealt with by a young monk who had traveled the familiar road from indulgence to fidelity and faith. American culture has always been captivated by visions of purity and by the proper harnessing of the energies of the spirit. "Waste not, want not" has been not only an adage for material advancement, but a way of responding to life as such and even to the possibilities of spiritual excellence.

The Seven Storey Mountain is an American *Pilgrim's Progress.* It serves in this capacity not only because of the introspective character of the search but because it deals effectively with the American temptation to substitute secular experience for spiritual substance. For many Americans the spiritual quest for worth becomes a secular need for achievement or excitement.

Commentators as diverse as Alexis de Tocqueville and F. Scott Fitzgerald have seen in the American hunger for affluence a need to be spiritually free rather than indulgently comfortable. Thomas Merton followed a path that made of privilege a peculiar kind of saving grace. He was born of artist parents, raised in an international environment, attended some of the best schools in Europe and America. But education and prestige, even talent and self-assertion, did not satisfy. Merton's autobiography reflects the middle-aged, middle-class ennui that came to other Americans later in life although for precisely the same reasons that affected this precocious young man.

It is intriguing to realize how closely Merton's work follows the conventions of Puritan autobiography. These required a description of wanton youthfulness, an adolescent conversion that does not endure, a mature commitment to faith, and a need to give witness by a written account that is part journal, part confession, and thoroughly didactic. Puritan autobiography, like *The Seven Storey Mountain,* works to dissipate illusion and to describe worldly life in stern and hostile terms.

Thomas Merton's journey from alleged deception to the rigors of "reality" in a pre-Vatican II Trappist monastery is a latter-day Puritan's progress. Puritans were obsessed, as was Merton, with the need to get beyond the shadow and the disguise, to achieve sincerity, to clarify perceptions of the world, to save others from pitfalls and wrong turns.

The Puritan analogs in Merton's work and career are abundant. Puritans were poets and essayists, preachers and teachers. Merton did his best work in these four areas. The autobiographical search for a self that would remain faithful despite fierce temptation was, for the Puritan, a public search, one that the convert was obliged to share with others.

The autobiographical poetry of Anne Bradstreet, the public confessional writings of the Mathers, the personal narratives of Jonathan Edwards, even the secular equivalent of all this in Benjamin Franklin, are not only part of American history, but early indications of a concern that has continued into the present. Ernest Hemingway and Thomas Wolfe, Norman Mailer and Saul Bellow, John Steinbeck and John Updike wrote novels that addressed the same issues. Like the Puritans before him, Merton begins his writing career as a poet, indeed as a religious poet.

The Puritan autobiographer made Providence the chief actor in the drama of life. Indeed, life was but a stage on which Providence acted through the self. Since the Puritans were Calvinists, they were terrified by the possibility of a universe that was not ordered. In their personal lives, they sought a pattern that would ensure the presence of grace and the benign purpose of a deity. Later Americans would also demand order in their world, but it would become an order imposed by their own wills and energy, by their efficiency and science. Self-reliance rather than divine action would become the means by which order would be achieved, but the need for an ordered world would be the same as that of the Puritans.

Merton was frightened by his own capacity for anarchy and indulgence. He required constraint and discipline to order his life. Had he not become a Trappist, he most likely would have dissipated his talent and destroyed his life. His conversion to Catholicism began the process of radically ordering his life. The conversion experience was intense; the church he joined, strict and authoritarian. But this was not enough.

Catholicism tends to be more demanding in its doctrinal expression than in the behavior it demands of its believing members. Reformed

Christianity, on the other hand, stresses moral rather than theological rectitude. Merton needed something or someone to order his personal life. The monastery offered him the discipline he required to save himself. It is doubtful he would ever leave monastic life, although he sometimes toyed with the idea. Intuitively he knew that without monasticism he would wander into futility. His vocation was a response both to God and to his own need to remain consistent with himself. Even as a hermit he maintained strong ties with his community and its superior.

The tension in Merton between anarchy and discipline proved creative. Too much of either would have destroyed him as an artist. The secret of his genius has something to do with balance between extremes. His writing is never worse than when he follows the strict rules of Scholastic theology or Cistercian piety. *The Ascent to Truth* and his biographies of Trappistine mystics are among his worst books.

As he breaks free of this rigidity into a spontaneity more his own, he writes poetry and theology in a more imaginative and ingenious manner. *The Geography of Lograire* and *Zen and the Birds of Appetite* may be the best work he ever did in either genre. If too much discipline would have destroyed his talent, his distinctive anarchy would also have limited his range and his vision. His writing appealed to so large an audience because there were passages in his books that both radicals and reactionaries found congenial.

Merton: The Beginnings

Merton, like many of the people of the century he lived in, felt out of place everywhere. "The sense of exile bleeds inside me like a hemorrhage," he confesses as a young man in *The Secular Journal.* "I don't know where to go, what to look for," he writes in his one published novel.[2] He was hardly able to walk when he was taken on a journey to find a new home across the Atlantic.

Thomas Merton was born on the last day of January in the first year of a world war, 1915. His parents were artists, Ruth Jenkins and Owen Merton, who had met in Paris. A year after their marriage, Ruth gave birth to Thomas in Prades, France.

Dislocation and tension on a global scale marked the first year of his life. There was anxiety caused by the proximity of the opposing armies. There was also a personal conflict between Ruth and Owen about the rightness of pacifism at a time of such calamity. Ruth was a Quaker; Owen felt obliged to enlist. As a New Zealander, he felt ties of loyalty to Britain. Many years later, his second son, John Paul, though an American, would serve with the Royal Canadian Air Force and lose his life in combat. In this, John Paul was like Owen. Many years later, Owen's first son, Thomas, would become a pacifist and protest against the many wars waged during his lifetime. In this, Thomas was like Ruth.

The contradictions that characterized Merton's life were already present in his parents. Owen was tolerant, laissez-faire; Ruth was intense, an intrepid journal-keeper and diarist. Ruth had a strong sense of herself that made adherence to formal religion distasteful. Owen saw in organized religion possibilities for personal growth and enrichment. Owen was a wanderer who did not require constant contact with a family, even his own, for survival. Ruth was rooted in relatives and sought ties with people.

Thomas hardly knew his mother and yet he was like her in many ways. She died when he was six years old, but her judgmental attitude lives on in *The Seven Storey Mountain.* Her fascination with journals continued in her son's brilliant use of this form of writing. Even if Thomas inherited many of his mother's traits, his love for her was not deep. It is quite possible that his father was the only person he fully trusted. Those he later loved as friends were reflections of a father from whom he was painfully separated before his sixteenth year was complete. Like Owen, Thomas was a wanderer.

Everyone in the immediate Merton family died young and tragically. Ruth died of cancer of the stomach; her husband, of a brain tumor. (Thomas worried throughout his life about his susceptibility to cancer.) John Paul died as a young airman; Thomas, of electrocution, at the height of his career. There were no children, no survivors. The immediate family had run its entire course in all its generations in approximately the life expectancy of a single person.

Thomas, born in France, as we have seen, of an American mother and a New Zealander father, was without nationality and without roots much of his life. This engendered in him a sense of exclusion, exile, and paradox. His childhood was not happy; the wildness of young adulthood was the symptom of an emptiness he could not fill. His life journey was both search and flight. He longed for home and yet felt strange everywhere. He fled from himself and his friends partly because he was restless, partly because he feared affection as much as he needed it, partly because he had so often been abandoned by those he loved.

Thomas was not always a victim in the search for abiding affection. He could become callous with others at times. He writes in an unpublished journal of his selfishness, of his inability to believe that women he loved could truly love him. There seems to be good evidence he abandoned a son and the child's mother in England when he came to New York. They were killed in World War II.[3] Again, war emerges as a shaper of his life, as a destroyer of those with whom he identified. The affair fueled the anger of his guardian and led to Thomas's removal from Cambridge and, remotely, to his vocation as a monk and mystic. Like St. Augustine before him, he sought rarer forms of purity and fidelity to compensate for the guilt he felt toward those he failed.

Merton was similar to Augustine in many ways. Both men developed their thought unsystematically and intuitively. Both were significantly identified by autobiographies. Each was responsible for a son born outside of marriage. Each underwent intense conversion experiences; in both cases, the conversion was consequent upon reading; in both cases, the person in question became a priest. Merton's abbot for most of his monastic career, James Fox, believes Merton modeled himself on Augustine and wrote as candidly as he did about himself because he sensed an affinity with Augustine. The similarities between Merton and Augustine were observed by early reviewers of *The Seven Storey Mountain,* though the affair we have alluded to had yet to be publicized fully.

Merton was a vulnerable man. This was his glory and his sorrow. His inability to love a woman faithfully convinced him that there was an incompleteness in him that could never be remedied. It led him to fall in love deeply in the later years of his life.[4] The idea of a contemplative and a hermit romantically in love makes Merton all the more a symbol of our era. It gives evidence to his human feeling and to the character of his spirituality. He moved away from relationship, but not easily and not without a sense of irreplaceable loss.

My Argument with the Gestapo

"The rocks cry out like glass," Merton writes in his novel *My Argument with the Gestapo.* The book offers insight into the life of a confused and searching young man—when he wrote it, Merton was twenty-six years of age. He writes about himself and the time immediately preceding America's entry into the Second World War.

The writing at times seems surrealistic: James Joyce and Franz Kafka are obvious influences. In the career of Merton, this autobiographical novel is the Joycean equivalent of *A Portrait of the Artist as a Young Man.*

Merton is bewildered. He is alienated, as was Joyce, from parents, native land, and religion. Yet one senses in the novel the expectation and excitement of a man who has not found his way but believes he will. He called the novel a journal when he brought it to a publisher in 1941; *Journal of My Escape from the Nazis.* It is indeed more a journal than a novel, closer to autobiography than to fiction.

In addition to the four earlier journals of Merton, (*The Secular Journal, The Sign of Jonas, Conjectures of a Guilty Bystander, The Asian Journal),* one must include among his major autobiographical writings *My Argument with the Gestapo, The Seven Storey Mountain,* and an epic poem, *The Geography of Lograire.* After Merton's death, volumes of his other journals were published.

It is not surprising that Merton would be confused at this point in his life. He was a child of the lost generation, an admirer of Ernest Hemingway, traveling the route from France to America rather than the reverse. The first voyage of his life, as an infant, was a frantic effort by his parents to escape a war that would soon engulf the Western world. The crossing of the Atlantic was accomplished on a ship mounted with a gun and with constant anxiety about U-boats.

Now Merton had lost both his parents, had been shuttled from the United States to France to England, had been forced out of Cambridge. He had been through a conversion experience, a number of failed love affairs, a fling with communism, some flirtation with nonviolence and Eastern spirituality, social work in Harlem, the beginning of a writing career, and the onset of the Second World War. He had tried everything and concluded that life never gives the pleasure it promises. One night, drunk on the floor of a Greenwich Village bar, he kept saying to his incredulous friends, "I'm going to be a priest, I'm going to be a priest."[5] Thomas Merton would not live life in a conventional manner.

In *My Argument with the Gestapo,* Merton writes in a manner reminiscent of the lostness and loneliness of Thomas Wolfe's prose:

> Someday, to this door, will come some person with the news I am waiting for, although I do not know what kind of news it is that I am waiting for.... I don't know what kind of person to look for, and I don't know what language I will hear spoken at the door....[6]

The novel is a story of guilt, the conjectures of a bystander who realizes that he is a participant in the evil of a war about to destroy the lives of millions. (The awareness that one must not act as though one had no part in the sins of one's own era pervades a later journal he writes, as he moves from monastic silence to social protest.) Like Robert Penn Warren in *All the King's Men,* written at about the same time, he makes it clear that all of us are both victims and perpetrators in the crimes of our generation. No one is guiltless.

The psychology of this intense young man explains in part the attraction he feels toward the priesthood and Cistercian life. He had not known normal home life. He misses his father desperately. He is lonely and confused. He has a strong sense of guilt about his sexual excesses, a guilt he suppresses with alcohol and wild behavior. He finds no pleasure in living, no enduring relationships, no clear sense of self.

He is also fired with idealism. He wants all women to be like Jinny Burton, the young woman he loves when he is a student at Columbia. Yet he cannot love her when they are together.[7] He wants a world of no more war, an Asian sense of tranquility. He identifies with the oppressed and the forsaken of the earth, He wants to become a great poet. He wishes to hear at the door a language he can comprehend.

Merton writes a novel, the only novel of his ever published, and he writes it about himself, about the world, and about the war, about the Nazis and about his vocation. He writes about writing, about all that it means to him. In a sense, he will be faithful to writing the way he was faithful to nothing else in his life. He writes at the end of his novel that his book is "as precious as an only child" and watches it leave him for a "terrible journey." The child is, of course, Merton, and the journey is the history of his life.

There are intriguing fragments and clues in the novel about deep psychic needs. The Hotel Rocamadour in which the fictional Merton resides in Paris is named after a Marian shrine Merton once visited with his father as a child. The reference is replete with meaning. France and his father represent roots and home. Both are lost to him now. Mary is the pure woman, the ideal, whom he seeks and does not find.

As Merton writes his novel, he is about to die to a former way of life, to enter a severe monastic community. The images that were most meaningful in his young life now cluster in his mind: France, father, Mary, childhood, Jinny Burton, writing, home. The fictional Merton has a passport issued by a country named "Casa," a reference undoubtedly to the home he never had and to the home he now seeks in the Abbey of Our Lady of Gethsemani.

My Argument with the Gestapo is Thomas Merton's farewell to the world. His disgust with the world is similar to Ezra Pound's style in *Hugh Selwyn Mauberley.* Pound is motivated by the waste of the First World War; Merton, by that of the Second. Merton, in a line reminiscent of Pound, writes: "They died for humor, and good sense, and even for sports."

The novel is a novel of fancy but everywhere there is the smell and taste of decay. The fictional Merton conducts an endless search by means of questions that receive no answers and by journeys that have no motive other than movement. There is a paralysis at the heart of the novel despite the frenzy on the surface and around the periphery. Many words are used but neither communication nor clarity emerge.

The main character is "Thomas Merton." He defines himself as a writer, seeking by words his proper place and adult responsibility in the scheme of things. The writing in the novel has warmth and personal character. Later, such writing will captivate a worldwide audience. The book shows a capacity for poetry, theology, and literary criticism; for autobiography that reveals not only himself but his contemporaries. The novel is not significant literature as a novel, but it is an impressive document for the interpretation of a significant writer. It is young in its enthusiasms and extravagant guilt, in its self-conscious attempts to be clever, and in its imitation of accepted literary masters. It is revealing of the present psychological state of the writer and of the future development of his thought.

The passion of the novel is for poetry and for nonviolence. The poetry shapes the structure and technique of the novel; the nonviolence provides substance and motive. Later, Merton will become both poet and prophet of pacifism. The novel is filled with longing, a longing expressed at times touchingly, as in the case of the anonymous woman dressed in uniform during the war. "As soon as she put on soft clothes again, she wanted to cry. Everywhere we go, in the parks, she looks for flowers…."[8] The novel is rich in humor and parody. A soldier describes "Thomas Merton" to his commanding officer:

> ….about twenty-six, light hair, blue eyes…. Talks a little like an American. Doesn't smoke, like Hitler: probably doesn't drink either. Doesn't like Cambridge, although I'm sure I can't say if that indicates anything.[9]

The novel presents Merton as a man of complexity and vitality, simultaneously hopeful and skeptical, filled with faith and fear, with ideals and suspicions. He shows a capacity for nonsense and solemnity, discipline and anarchy. His career would indeed be interesting to watch unfold. In retrospect, one realizes that the main elements of his future life are present from the beginning.

One of the unexpected aspects of the life of Merton is his consistency. To the casual observer he seems erratic. Beneath the surface divergencies, however, there are striking similarities. The interest in poetry is lifelong. The concern with peace emerges on a grand scale in the 1960s, but it is present as a commitment in the young man. Human rights for black Americans are a cause he espouses in the 1930s as well as in the 1950s. His attraction to mysticism is present in his magisterial thesis on William Blake as well as, much later in life, when he writes of Zen Buddhism.

Few things troubled Merton as much as safe solutions to perplexing problems. In a letter to Mark Van Doren, his professor at Columbia as well as a friend, he writes: "the safe I can no longer stomach." This distrust of the status quo would lead him later to become a significant influence in ecclesial renewal, Cistercian reform, and social revolution. Merton wanted to transcend arbitrary human limitations and thereby become a universal symbol. He wanted to harmonize in himself East and West, past and present, secular and sacred. He said this time and again in so many words.

One might consider this desire egocentric, but one must also consider the candor with which he discussed his failings, even the failings unknown to others. He observes in an unpublished journal, one he had intended eventually to publish, that he had written enough to destroy his reputation. He was unwilling to receive commendation in excess of the merits of his achievements. He writes to Boris Pasternak that he is a minor poet. He judges a number of his books inferior or even awful.

Vocation and Commitment

On December 9, 1941, two days after the attack on Pearl Harbor, a young man boards a train in the winter darkness and begins the long ride to Gethsemani. He has just resigned his position in the English department at St. Bonaventure College in New York. There is freezing rain as the train pulls out of Olean. He is on his way to become a Trappist monk.

The paradox is not yet apparent. The journey into solitude and anonymity is the first step into fame and renown. The vocation that was to take him out of the world, so to speak, would bring him into much sharper contact with it. By comparison, the life he had lived so far, a life in which one was expected to develop reputation and prominence, was a life of obscurity.

The dark hills are barely visible as winter rain streaks the windows of the train. Later, much later, as a hermit in the woods of Gethsemani, he would write eloquently of the rain and the dark hills of Kentucky.

It snowed the day he was born. That was so unusual an occurrence in Prades, France, that the newspapers made much of it. He was born at nine-thirty at night. It was night now as he prepared for another birth. His life seemed bound to autumn and winter. He was born in January and he was to die in early December. He was born on a street named September (1 Rue du 4 Septembre); he entered Gethsemani in December. The weather was harsh once again on February 2, 1915, when Owen took his infant son to register him according to French law, at the mayor's office. The name was "Tom" on his birth certificate; his mother insisted it not be "Thomas."

Strange the things one remembers as a former way of life dies. The train roars through Buffalo, Erie, Cleveland, and pulls into Cincinnati at dawn.

How did all this vocation business begin? His father did something unusual on his deathbed: he started to draw figures he had never sketched before. Owen Merton was a landscape painter; in his final illness, however, he sketched Byzantine saints. Later, Thomas would become a monk drawn to the East and to Byzantine Christianity. When Thomas himself dies in Bangkok, the American Embassy lists among his effects a Byzantine icon. He had carried it halfway around the world into the mystery of his own death. As Owen Merton dies, something deep in his psyche turns him to the East. His son would follow the same route and die there.

Perhaps the vocation began in the churches of Rome. The city fascinated him. He was haunted by the Byzantine mosaics and sought out the churches that contained them. Although he was not aware of this, the mosaics seemed to affect him because of the figures he had seen his father draw. He became a pilgrim and prayed in a church for the first time in his life at the Church of Santa Sabina in Rome. At this time he underwent a strange experience. The young Thomas Merton was alone in his room at night, with the light on, when his father, now deceased a year, flashed into his sight. Stirred to the depths of his being, he prayed and wept.

Although Merton was an impressionable person, he had an antipathy for anything connected with communication with the dead. He attributed the incident to his imagination or to a psychological disturbance within him. The experience had a profound effect on him; he recalled it in vivid detail years later. Not long after, the young Merton visits the Trappist monastery at Tre Fontane in Rome. He walks under the trees nearby for a long time that afternoon. The thought strikes him that he would like to become a Trappist monk. Merton is not a Catholic, yet he thinks of monasticism. Little more than a year after his father's death, Merton goes to Rome, prays, begins a conversion experience, and contemplates a monastic vocation. It is a psychologically turbulent time, a creative and dramatic beginning to a new form of life.

His memories shift. The memories are not now those of sight but of sound. "*Yo creo,*" he hears, and remembers the cry from a liturgy he attended in Cuba. A Franciscan brother had begun the Creed and a chorus of children thundered, *"Creo en Dios."* That moment he experienced God so deeply that all previous and most subsequent encounters paled by comparison. Now, less than two years later, Merton is on a train to Gethsemani. His father appeared to him as light in Rome. God was a blinding light in Cuba. The train pulls into Cincinnati in the pale light of a new day. He changes trains for the final stage of the journey to Louisville and Gethsemani.

It was but a week ago that he was standing in the darkness listening to a bell ring in his memory. He had tried to knock at the door of a priest who might finally assure him that his vocation made sense. Every time he put his hand on the door he was seized by paralysis and fear. He felt exhausted, confused, depressed. He ran out into the rain and in the night silence heard the bell of Gethsemani ring. It would be ringing at Gethsemani at that precise moment, but the abbey was hundreds of miles away. He had heard that bell often when on retreat in Gethsemani. Now it emerged in his consciousness and exploded in his memory with such a force that he lost his hesitation. In his novel, he had wondered about the door that would open and the language people would speak on the other side. The language this time was the language of acceptance.

It all fused together now: Rome and Cuba, creeds and bells. There was no turning back. The vocation was certain; the decision was made.

And now the train ride. A strange feeling of peace and joy. The mystery of it all. That Thomas Merton should be in such a situation. From Byzantine sketches made by a mute, dying father to a bell that sounded deep inside him and summoned him to a journey, to a new sense of himself. The train ride into an unfamiliar experience was bringing him home. The idea of being home was as tentative as the excursion into the unknown. He had known so little warmth in his life. Why did he fear the affection he needed? Why did he forever keep people at a distance with his humor, his unconventional behavior, his perverse tendency to do something that would confound their expectations and unsettle them with its unconventionality? Was he becoming a Trappist for such reasons?

This new journey could work only if it would prove to be a journey into compassion. He needed more sensitivity to others. He always worried about that. Buddhism would later interest him, because of its stress on compassion. He could be so rough with others, so harsh.

The last poem he wrote in his life was an epic about the failure of human relationships and about himself. He called it *The Geography of Lograire.* It was not like anything else he had written. He was different now at the end from what he was at the beginning. Or, at least, most thought so. The poem is a puzzle, like the man and the century. It is more intractable than *The Seven Storey Mountain* and yet similar to it in its exploration of the self and the meaning of the self in the light of the age. He was now an enigma. People were no longer sure of what he might do next.

On the train ride, however, he seems sure. He wishes to become a Trappist, to leave the world, to get as far from New York as possible, to atone for his past life, to encounter God. Twenty-three years later he returns to New York. In 1941 he departs from New York anonymously; in 1964 he comes back as the most celebrated monk since Martin Luther. A world celebrity. Isn't that something he always wanted? The return to New York was exhilarating. Columbia University. Harlem. Zen Buddhism. D.T. Suzuki. The return trips are fascinating barometers of change in the man. The difference twenty-three years makes is monumental.

The trips to New York are real. One can also see the change in the man by considering the two trips he takes to Japan. These are not trips actually taken. They are taken in his mind and present in his writing. The first book about Japan is *Exile Ends in Glory;* the second, *Zen and the Birds of Appetite.* He writes the first book in 1948; the second in 1968.

Exile Ends in Glory. Not a bad title for his life. But the book is not about him. Indeed, it hardly seems to be a book by him. He is a young monk. Later he evaluates the book as "bad." He is right. The theology is worse than the story. He is narrow, arrogant.

The book is about a woman. He never writes well of women. It is the biography of a Trappist nun, Mother M. Berchmans. He writes the book because his superior assigns it to him. The second book on Japan will be one many of his superiors would have preferred he did not write. But, at the moment, it is 1948 and Merton is not sure about what he should write or how. He yearns to write. Hagiography becomes a way he can allow himself to be both submissive and self-assertive, responsive to the Trappist tradition and to his abbot, and yet a writer, following a career he always wanted. The compromise does not work. Writing never does when it is a compromise.

The God presented in *Exile Ends in Glory* favors bitter austerity, grim isolation, discipline, pain. The trials expected of a young girl in the narrative and the approval of them by the young monk who writes of her are humanly cruel and spiritually counterproductive. She is expected to wash pigs to learn humility, to wear bells on her fingers to retrain gesticulation, to punish herself with whips, to stifle every effort to laugh.

A mistress of novices orders that each nun limit correspondence with parents not only to infrequent intervals but also with regard to length. No more than two pages will be permitted. These, of course, will be read by superiors. When Berchmans explains that her family will think she cares for them less if her letters become markedly brief, she is told she may write letters of three pages, in honor of the Trinity. The young woman is permitted to write a longer letter for the sake of the number three but not for human love or affection. Merton does not object.

Later, Merton will protest against arbitrary and inhuman spiritual norms. But he is not ready yet for such objections. The young monk is rigid. He rebukes the subject of his biography when she is capricious enough to believe God will not punish her eternally in hell if she misses chanting the prayers of the Office once. Merton goes on to condemn the France Berchmans left as a country of "mean and crafty bureaucrats," of "little fat atheists with fake teeth" who read newspapers through "weak spectacles" and "betray their civil marriages with cynical and regular openness."[10] There is no doubt the young man can write. One does, however, wonder about his judgment.

If France is bad, Japan is worse. Japan is denounced as a land of pagans whose spirituality is superstitious. Berchmans lives in Japan and despises the culture. Merton approves. The Japanese offer incense to "blind, dead wayside gods of bronze." Twenty years later in Ceylon (Sri Lanka) Merton will behold the Buddha in ecstasy. Now, however, the culture is dismissed imperiously. The Japanese were

> crippled by appalling pagan hatreds and lusts and envies and dark superstitions and despairs from which they had no way of freeing themselves. All their movements, all their attempts, only seemed to entangle them more in the great web of sins woven by centuries of paganism and idolatry.[11]

They are destined to "fall like plummets into the depths of hell." The cultural and religious arrogance is exceeded only by the defective theology. Merton observes that Jesus had seen the Japanese "as He lay in the manger at Bethlehem. Christ had seen them all as he worked at the bench in Joseph's shop." The christology is sentimental. It exceeds, furthermore, a respect for the limits of the humanity of Christ, a humanity violated by imposing upon the human the prerogatives of divinity.

Twenty years after *Exile Ends in Glory,* Thomas Merton journeys to Japan again in his great book, *Zen and the Birds of Appetite.* It is not the same man. It does not even seem to be the same century. Now Japanese culture and spirituality are absolutely indispensable for the enrichment of Christianity and for the maturity of the West.

So many trips. So many journeys.

Journeys. Circles. Labyrinths. Rings encircling the mountain—seven storeys of them. No summits. Footpaths forever. Depressing plateaus. Painful ascents. Ascent to truth. Precarious ledges. No man is an island—the impossible island. Crevices. Diminishing treelines. Pitfalls. Plane flights and train rides. How many times across the Atlantic? The Pacific only once. Too many journeys. Japan was on the itinerary after Bangkok. After Bangkok, nothing—everything.

But now we are on a train—to Gethsemani. Or, better, we are in the land of Lograire, the geography of his last poem. More precisely, we are in the North canto of the poem. More specifically, we are in the Queens

Tunnel. Thomas Merton is a boy and New York terrifies him. It is the funnel-tunnel, as he calls it. The smokestack of death and the canal of life. "Life and death are even." "My Lady Mum is all alive." Later she will die, of course, and the smoke from her burned body will dissipate in the chimney. She disappears in a funnel whose body was the tunnel that gave him life. Mother, hear me sing my "orange song." She did not seem to love him, and he never got over the lack. Is this why he now goes to Gethsemani?

He is a boy in the land of Lograire. A boyhood in Queens. But Queens does not save. "Most holy incense burners of Elmhurst save us." His mother does not save him. She dies. He never was a child really. And the girl was more than all the rest: "I met her by the lamp. We swam in ginger ale." It was exhilarating. But it was over. Merton was "alone under the maple." "I cannot come, I said. I have dead people to attend to." When he writes this poem, his mother, his father, his brother are dead. His death will keep him from completing the poem.

The North canto is a meditation on death. This train ride to Gethsemani is also a journey into death. In Lograire, there is only the underworld of Homer and Virgil and Dante where the dead somehow survive. But also the underworld of Mafia and spies. New York is a world of "subways," the "undertow of a big city." If only he could get free of the unhappiness and the frantic pace, free of "the spinning winter bridges, the lovelorn whooping crane...the wine-garbage waters..." There is the death of someone Merton calls "my baby" and the death of a "Bonnie... laid out on a long white table." He sits down and weeps. The world is dying. There are race wars and police states, military engagements and urban decay. "Geography is in trouble all over Lograire."

The poem we are discussing comes late in the life of Merton, but the events it recounts are present in his memory as he journeys to

Gethsemani. There is sexual attraction in the poem also. A "Lois" and the poet are young enough "to act foolish." He tells "Ruthie" that another love, "the grey-eyed Church," has won his affection. There are also "Anna" and "Connie." Some of the sexual references are savage and intertwine with the theme of death and the brutality of the city.

Kitty is raped in the streets of New York as people pretend not to notice. The flight of Kitty through the city is a flight into death. She is surrounded by guilty bystanders but no saviors. Flight becomes another form of death. Rivers run; buses speed; police cars race; planes hover. The city is not a city of residents but of "passengers." Movement, flight, journey, pilgrimage. The world is frantic with migrations. From the East River to the Thames, there is no peace; from Queens to Cambridge, the world is restless.

The train stops. It is quiet. He is in love. It is a different love. He walks to the gate of the abbey. He rings the bell that will give him entrance. The bell. He heard it so clearly last week. A brother opens the door. And Thomas Merton walks inside. Not a tunnel this time. A garden. His young heart is overwhelmed. He thought he would never make it home.

The Prose and Poetry of Life

Prose was not his native medium. He was a man of symbols rather than sentences, better with metaphors than with method. His journals were effective because they had an episodic, epigrammatic, elusive quality more congenial to verse than to conventional writing. In both the prose and the poetry, the journey motif dominates.

The journey of Thomas Merton was not only the journey of a life, but a journey through the century. He makes contact in his writing with the cataclysmic events of his era: world wars and nuclear arsenals, social violence and Church reform, cultural upheavals and social revolutions. Tranquility is not easy in such a time, even for a hermit. Perhaps it is not even desirable. To touch a tortured age, one must absorb its pain. Healing is the gift of the wounded. The journey through the twentieth century must pass through its afflictions. A Passover journey does not omit the desert or the cross, the exile or the dying.

Merton was convinced that the suffering required for sanctity in a secular age must originate with the pain of the world. The discipline that is demanded is identification with the anguish of the world in its search for meaning.

The spirituality of Thomas Merton is shaped not only by ecclesiastical culture but by a secular era; not only by Cistercian traditions but by contemporary tensions; not only by monastic environment but by a mundane climate. The journey of Merton is, paradoxically, a journey all can recognize as their own, even though the form it takes is remote and inaccessible to the lives of most people. It is not the character of the search but the motive and the meaning that matter. In the habit of a Trappist monk, a brother was present to us, someone whose age and preoccupations were the same as our own.

Whether Thomas Merton writes of the Queens Tunnel or the Columbia campus, the French countryside or Cambridge University, the Abbey of Gethsemani or the hill-hidden hermitage, he writes of us.

Merton's capacity to reflect the century in which he lives is reminiscent of John Henry Newman in the century before him. The lives of both men were characterized by intense, internal journeys. In many aspects their lives were comparable.

One of the most influential moments in the career of John Henry Newman occurred in Sicily. He had completed a trip to Rome and was shaken by the experience. For a reason he could not comprehend, he felt a need to remain in Italy, to separate himself from his traveling companions, to be alone in Sicily. An experience of beauty and terror followed in rapid succession. He visited Taormina and thought it the most beautiful place on earth. Soon after, he almost died, stricken with a fever and delirium so severe that he viewed his recovery as a resurrection from the dead. In his journals, he describes vividly his cries in the grip of an intense physical and spiritual struggle: "I have not sinned against the light!" On the way home from Sicily, he composed at sea the famous poem concerning his search and his sense of a destiny beyond his knowing: "Lead, Kindly Light."

It was in Italy that Thomas Merton was also changed by a profound experience. We have seen how Byzantine mosaics in Rome stirred him, bringing to the surface in a way he could not comprehend the death of his father and the enigmatic sketches on his deathbed. He, too, was painfully ill on this journey, from blood poisoning, and he was alone. Merton also had a vision of light and became conscious of sin in its presence. His experience with this light made him want to sin against it no more. The need for purity led him to Catholicism, monasticism, priesthood, contemplation, the hermitage. It sent him on a journey through the centuries to the desert fathers and to the East, where he saw again the light he had been seeking. The sun shone on his death in the afternoon, a death caused by an electric current that blazed forth and burned him.

In Rome, Thomas Merton prayed formally for the first time in his life. He, too, said things he could not comprehend. At the Trappist monastery in Rome he spoke of wanting to be a Trappist monk although he was neither Catholic nor attracted to Catholicism. He did not want to sin against the light or to miss his destiny. This much was clear to him, but what this all meant or how it would work its way out he did not know.

The lives of John Henry Newman and Thomas Merton are divided chronologically by decisive conversion experiences at midpoint.

Newman enters the Catholic Church in his forty-fifth year of life; he dies at the age of eighty-nine. Turning back from that experience and his life in that Church was unthinkable to him.

The final stages of Merton's conversion reach their development at the age of twenty-six, when he rings the bell at Gethsemani and asks to be admitted as a member of the community; he dies at the age of fifty-three. Turning back from that experience was not unthinkable for Merton, but it was, as far as we can judge, something he would never actually do. Fidelity to God as well as to himself required from each man a permanent commitment to the conversion experience begun in Rome. There would be many changes for both as their careers progressed, but the framework in which these changes would be given consistency was set by the dramatic changes at midpoint in each of their lives.

Both men were influenced by Augustine. Like him, each wrote a famous autobiography: *Apologia pro Vita Sua* in Newman's case; *The Seven Storey Mountain* in Merton's. Augustine's autobiography was the story of a spiritual journey, a journey that moved his life in a direction which neither his previous dispositions nor his future expectations indicated. The *Apologia* is the story of a spiritual journey that takes Newman reluctantly in a direction his training as an Anglican priest and his emotional nature neither foresee nor prefer. Merton's reading of Aldous Huxley and Etienne Gilson began his conversion to Catholicism. *The Seven Storey Mountain* describes the spiritual journey that brings Merton to a point neither he nor his friends could have anticipated. Merton's first contact with the East is through the Hindu monk Bramachari, who suggests that he read not a book of Asian spirituality, but the *Confessions* of St. Augustine.

Newman and Merton were deeply interested in the Patristic Age, especially in those manifestations of Christianity that preceded Scholasticism and centralization in Rome. Both men were suspect by Church administrators. Indeed, Merton's attraction to Newman was intensified about the time he himself was silenced by Church authorities on the issue of peace. He was angered at what Newman had suffered at the hands of the hierarchy and felt himself also a victim of administrative chicanery.

Neither Newman nor Merton was creative theologically or aesthetically in the context of Thomistic thought or official doctrine. In an *Essay on the Development of Christian Doctrine* and *An Essay in Aid of Grammar of Assent,* Newman was very much his own man. His thinking exceeded Scholastic confines and official Church teaching. In *Conjectures of a Guilty Bystander, Zen and the Birds of Appetite,* and *The Geography of Lograire,* Merton achieved the same freedom. Both men were thinkers attuned to poetry and to the heart: *Cor ad cor loquitur*—heart speaks to heart.

Newman and Merton had a sense of the importance of their lives and of their need to preserve carefully the records of their activities and thought. Newman was the more sentimental of the two.

A striking similarity between the two men is obvious in the influence their undergraduate education had upon them. For Newman, Oxford was an emotional and a life experience. He became a fellow of one of its colleges, with the intention of remaining there for life. For Merton, Columbia represented some of the happiest years of his life. It was the only educational institution he felt attracted to during his sometimes unhappy years in schooling. He went from Columbia into teaching with the intention of making it a career. The closest friends in the lives of both men were the friends they made at their respective universities. Their thought was indelibly shaped by those early, warm, and enduring associations.

We have had occasion to note that both found the autobiographical form of writing congenial. They wrote famous autobiographies.

They were poets, and their poetry contains a significant autobiographical component. They were novelists; their novels are about events and experiences in their own lives. Newman writes of his young manhood in the novel *Loss and Gain;* Merton does the same in *My Argument with the Gestapo.* Their writing is an effort not to promote themselves but to maintain their integrity and to grow spiritually.

Their journals are confessional, filled with a candor about their failures and a degree of honesty few people could manage. Critics of Newman's life are aware of his weaknesses because he detailed them so carefully himself. Merton realizes that his journals contain enough information to destroy his reputation. Neither man seemed comfortable having others think him better than he was.

For these and many other reasons, Merton is an American Newman, a twentieth-century version of the nineteenth-century master. The parallels are not perfect, obviously, but the convergences are significant. There are more than biographical similarities.

Newman and Merton reach the same audience with roughly the same effect. They lead their readers into new versions of the previous history and future possibilities of the Christian tradition. They encourage a dynamic rather than a static approach to the human and religious problems of their day. Merton does not have the theological genius of Newman; Newman lacks the social justice consciousness of Merton. Newman reaches primarily an academic, intellectual, Anglo or Roman Catholic audience. Merton appeals to the activist and the humanist, to the establishment but also to the periphery. Newman is by far the more accomplished writer; Merton is, perhaps, the better poet. If we wish to study nineteenth- or twentieth-century Catholic thought we could hardly do better than to consider in depth the lives of these two men whose biographies become the record of their era.

The sensitivity each showed toward his age is striking. Newman writes of the development of doctrine in an evolutionary frame of reference a decade and a half earlier than Charles Darwin's landmark theory. He analyzes faith from a psychological perspective as a convergence of probabilities rather than of absolute certitudes, and he does this a generation earlier than the work of Sigmund Freud on psychoanalysis.

Newman was profoundly sensitive to ecumenism, a movement that would begin to grip the Christian world in the decades following his death. He represents the end of the Cartesian-Newtonian mechanistic and mathematical approach to reality, and moves in the direction of the ambiguous and the probable, the indeterminate and the relative. He does this because he embodies the dynamism of his own era.

Merton is also prescient and sensitive. He deals with the fusion of contemplation and social action years before turbulent prophetic protest racks America. He envisioned a global system of social justice where racism and militarism were eliminated, where technology and affluence were relied on less for the solution of human problems. He offered spiritual and contemplative alternatives a generation before they became widely discussed possibilities for the enrichment of life.

He struggles with the difficult area where the claims of authority and the prerogatives of conscience intersect. He does this almost from the beginning of his monastic life, but most assuredly some fifteen years before the conclusion of the Second Vatican Council. He speaks of some atheists as secular mystics and of Asian religions as sources of grace and truth long before it became fashionable to so regard them. Merton explores the relationship between the secular and the sacred and between East and West as the twentieth century becomes fascinated with the correspondence between church and world, and with the compatibility of divergent cultural and religious systems.

Both Newman and Merton were artists. They wrote significant literature as well as incisive theology. They were able to discuss with equal ease Church history, the Patristic Era, literary criticism, theological systems, the poetry of their day, the major thinkers in belief systems not their own. They labored to write well and to think clearly, to refine their prose and polish their poetry, to discover a language their contemporaries could recognize as their own. They read newspapers and magazines voraciously, received visitors from every walk of life, and became prominent men in the development of the cultural and social histories of their nations.

Theology and Journey

We have touched on Merton's travels from France to England to America to Asia. *The Asian Journal* gives us a striking indication of how far he had come theologically from the narrow and arrogant judgments of his earlier years. He expressed himself then in categories that later embarrassed him. There was no possibility of changing his past, perhaps not even a need to do so. The task now was the transformation of the past by transcending it. The survival of the past could be accomplished by a discreet turning from it.

In the earlier days the theological correlations were narrow. In *The Living Bread,* he writes quite simply that Jesus lives in the world only because there are Catholic priests to ensure Christ's survival. Such a statement today astonishes and disappoints. It reduces the reality of Jesus to what is considered the larger reality of the Church. It limits the vitality of Christ to one group in the Church. It exalts the ordained ministry to a position more crucial than that of Christ. It makes the Christ of history and the Christ of the world dependent upon Catholics and clerics only.

Later, however, he writes in a more sophisticated way about the power and supremacy of a God whose freedom affirms us, grounds our freedom, and challenges our limits. Merton was always better when his categories were dialectical rather than dogmatic. It was a long theological journey, however, from a Christ made subject to the control and competence of priests to a God whose loftiness eludes and encounters us at the same time.

At the beginning of the theological journey, again in *The Living Bread,* the presence of Christ in the Eucharist is deemed essential if the Mass is to be anything more than a pious ceremony. The fact that the Mass would still be significant as a prayer even if there were no sacramental presence does not occur to Merton. Eucharistic presence has as its liturgical alternative, for him, empty ritual. Much later, Merton would appreciate the spiritual character of any ceremony that adequately expressed faith and seeks love. Indeed, at this early date, the presence of Christ in the Eucharist is limited to the explanation provided by transubstantiation. Christ is present in a state of sacrifice with all his sense faculties intact. Merton is even more conservative than the state of Catholic theology at that time.

In Merton's theology, the reality of the Eucharist is seen exclusively in terms of Christ's presence rather than correlatively in terms of a community's faith. The state of sacrifice or the character of the species or the integrity of Christ's reality are far more decisive for him than the act of faith or the quality of a congregation's participation. Christ is so conceived that the subtleties of interpersonal presence are disregarded for a concentration on the capacity of Jesus to exercise his sense faculties in the Eucharist. Merton is, of course, not alone responsible for this inadequate theology, but he is obviously not the critic of arbitrary faith or peripheral piety that he later becomes.

As time passes, Merton's concern is not with certitude or simple definitions, not even with answers. He moves from question to question. In *Faith and Violence,* he finds conventional approaches to God embarrassing; the Church is judged as seriously out of contact with modern life. Life is more nuanced, indeed, tragic. He has made contact with the pain. And he grows. "We huddle in the pale light of an insufficient answer to a question we're afraid to ask," he observes in *No Man Is an Island.*

In the early days, truth is easily packaged and quickly defined. "For outside the *Magisterium* directly guided by the Spirit of God we find no such contemplation and no such union with Him—only the void of Nirvana or the feeble intellectual light of Platonic idealism, or the sensual dreams of the Sufis."[12] Jesus was subject to priests, as we have seen before; now contemplative life is subject to the bishops. All other religious traditions are spiritually bankrupt.

In Asia, however, he is convinced that Christians and especially monks can improve the quality of their lives by making contact with Buddhism or Hinduism. Standing before the Buddhas at Polonnaruwa he enters into contemplation:

> I know and have seen what I was obscurely looking for. I don't know what else remains but I have now seen and pierced through the surface and have got beyond the shadow and the disguise.[13]

Thomas Merton journeyed a long road from the days of his simple Eucharistic piety and the unsophisticated hagiography of *Exile Ends in Glory.* He writes the above lines in the week of his death.

In the early *Seeds of Contemplation,* faith is "first of all an intellectual ascent." This view of faith restricts the equally important intuitive and emotional dimensions of faith. It diminishes the risk and courage of belief. It gives priority to the doctrinal component of faith and its institutional definition. In his personal life, Thomas Merton did not act out the stilted theology he repeats. At this point, however, Merton abides by theological formulas he does not accept at a more profound level of his life.

Obedience rather than inner conviction is the motivating force behind many of his statements, even though he accepts them at face value. He is insecure in his new faith and his new vocation. He therefore defines himself in ways that are sanctioned by those who seem to know better. The dynamism of his personality, his faith experience, his critical mind will later change the character of his thinking. In *The Asian Journal,* it is not certitude but being a marginal person that matters; it is not arrival but pilgrimage that counts; he comes to the East not to teach but to learn, not to intellectualize faith but to participate in "vision and experience." He is excited not by doctrinal definition but by the possibility he might attain complete Buddhahood, not after death, but even "in this life."

Once he had reasoned, impossibly, that "all our sanctity depends" on Mary, and even that Christ's suffering on the cross could be alleviated by our present response to it. In both cases, human life is considered in a highly abstracted fashion. God becomes essentially dependent upon Mary, and Christ on the cross is envisioned not as truly human and limited but as capable of experiencing the compassion of people who live many centuries later. At a future point in Merton's life, sanctity will be seen as a human engagement with the concrete issues of the day and with the world's anguish. He becomes enamored of an observation of Albert Camus's criticizing faith that took thinking down endless corridors of abstraction "without taking the trouble to notice that it was being unfaithful to changing situations and to the truth of the momentary context."

Merton is now a hermit near death. The long journey has been a pilgrimage to compassion. Even if others fault him, he at least did not "take the road to another man's city." His personal integrity is intact. The journey was not, however, as erratic or as eclectic or even as personal as it may have seemed. He followed a destiny more than he set his own course. The journey was "guided and directed," he knew, despite the false starts and crushing experiences en route.

Unusual dreams continued to disturb him. He never found the woman he desired or the Church he needed. He learned to settle for the lack, for the deficiency, for the absence, for the stupidity as well as the splendor of the Church, for the elusiveness as well as the proximity of God. Contemplation helped him to appreciate the ambiguities and the emptiness of fullness. This was, after all, only his first lifetime. There would be further journeys, other kingdoms, different cities. There are times when we must let the end be so that the beginnings get a chance. In Asia "the journey is only begun." It makes sense to end it there also.

Almost to the last day he asks, "Am I part of it?" He reaches for the other side of the contradiction, for the face of the mountain he cannot see. The dreams and questions are alive as he reaches for the fan in his room. The journey had gone on for so long that death was the only answer that remained. But death answers nothing. It merely poses a further question. He died convinced that the settling of "the great affair" had something to do with "going home." He was ready now, for the end and the beginning. The pilgrimage never ends; only particular paths terminate.

CHAPTER TWO

A Vow of Conversation

He was a Catholic writer whose worst writing was Catholic writing. Yet Catholicism was necessary to the development of his artistic talent.

The anarchy that seized his spirit at times afflicted his writing as well. He was a man who needed discipline, an extraordinary amount of it, for the refinement of his life and for the fulfillment of his calling as an artist.

As with so many other realities in his life, a dialectic was crucial for his growth. He needed Catholicism as a counterpoint, a polarity, a profound experience but not as a total system. His proximity to and independence from official Catholic teaching provided a creative dimension to his work. The early books, the most Catholic, required less creative energy and were, consequently, less original.

Writing was the most central of his many vocations. He need not have become a Catholic or a Trappist. But writing was a need over which he had no control. It complicated his life immeasurably, but he had no alternative.

He was once given a psychological self-identity test by young monks in his charge. The point of the test was to define oneself immediately after uttering the words "I am…" His first reaction was: "I am Thomas Merton, the famous author."[14] There is a world of meaning in this simple sentence. Writing and publishing were his essence. He does not identify himself first as a Catholic or a priest, as a monk or a contemplative, as a teacher or counselor. He is an author. Nothing pleases him more than to be regarded as a writer. But the writing is only part of it; the fame the writing brings matters as much. He wished to be celebrated even as he desired anonymity. The very fact that he does not identify himself by his religious name, Fr. Louis, but rather by his birth name, Thomas Merton, is an indication of how distinct his vocation as a writer was from his monastic commitment.

The need for recognition was not the same as a need for public attention. He desired the renown because he needed to touch people through his writing. The fame was his way of assuring himself that he could connect. In books, it was possible for him to make the offer of himself even at the deepest levels of his psyche without risking face-to-face rejection. There was the safe distance provided by the medium of print and the greater remoteness of his monastic seclusion and of his eremitical isolation.

In his books, he could be himself, wildly, joyously, totally. His autobiography was transparent in its candor; his journals, daring in their revelations. His acceptance, by so many people, at so many levels, in so many languages, with so much of himself revealed, was the evidence he required to believe he was worthwhile. Without the writing, he would have failed as a monk. The fact that his superiors prohibited him from joining the even more secluded Camaldolese or Carthusian communities—communities that would not have allowed a writing career—may have preserved his monastic vocation in a way it was difficult for him to appreciate.

The contradiction was never resolved. He sought silence more deeply as he matured in the contemplative life; he struggled to reach an audience more touchingly as he grew in his craft as a writer. Those who knew him best were those who read his books. They knew him better than those he taught or those with whom he lived. Merton's abbot and confessor, Flavian Burns, knew the man more clearly from his books than from personal contact.[15] This is simply astonishing as one reflects on it. Writing made the spirit of Merton real and tangible. It enabled him to be touched so that he might be set free.

The need to write was so great a hunger that it led to excess. His writing became repetitive; his ideas, so quickly developed that they canceled one another out at times. Yet his writing was carefully and frequently revised. The problem was not the lack of care but the impossibility of pausing in his writing. There seemed to be a compulsion at the root of the need, a compulsion that alarmed his friends and colleagues.

A group of these friends arranged for him to meet the great psychiatrist Gregory Zilboorg. Under the pretext of attending a conference on psychology and religion at St. John's University in Minnesota in 1956, Merton encountered Zilboorg. The purpose of this meeting was to restrain Merton from writing; he never learned in his lifetime that the meeting had been prearranged and that it had a hidden agenda.

Zilboorg saw Merton with the supposed purpose of discussing an article Merton had written on neurosis in religious life. Zilboorg accused Merton of a number of serious emotional deficiencies. He told him he was unsettled, a burden to his superiors, a gambler of sorts. Merton was guilty of a dialogue with Zen Buddhism that did not have conversion as its object. He was told he was an exhibitionist, that he believed his writing to be more important than it was, that he desired to live as a hermit solely for the attention it would bring him. Zilboorg informed Merton he would never last as a hermit unless the hermitage were located in the middle of Times Square, garishly illumined by a neon sign reading "Hermit lives here."

Merton was stunned. He began to weep and shout back in anger. Abbot James Fox recalls the meeting as one in which Merton collapsed more completely than he had ever seen a man collapse under a verbal assault.[16]

Merton later accepted the situation without rancor. He prayed that, if Zilboorg were correct, he might be healed.

The incident is remarkable because of the reaction it produced in Merton. The reader may make his or her own private judgment about the propriety, the mechanics, and the motives of the meeting. The reaction of Merton is of greater concern. The reaction was strong, I believe, because writing was more critical to his identity than any other commitment of his life. He had finally resolved after years of tension the appropriateness of continuing a writing career as a Trappist. Once this issue had been settled, words poured out of him because of the previous repression of his talent. He felt a furious need to express himself and to compensate for the lost years and the lost books, some of which had been burned when zeal and a desire to break with the past motivated him too ardently.

Zilboorg called his writing incoherent, using the term *babalogical* to dismiss it as little more than babble. No charge against a writer could be more devastating. Zilboorg told Merton the article on neurosis in religious life was so bad that revision was out of the question. He reduced Merton's vocation to exhibitionism. This included the yearning he felt to become a hermit and the commitment he made to writing. All this was done not sensitively or even alone but in the presence of Merton's very critical abbot, James Fox.

Something deep in the psyche of Thomas Merton was disturbed by the encounter. The most anguished moments in his life had been those when his life as a writer was called into question. In the beginning, the questioning was self-inflicted; later, criticisms emerged from others, some of whom proved to be censors as well. Finally, pressures were directed against him from his own community or from well-meaning but perhaps short-sighted friends or professionals.

In the main, Merton's Trappist community supported his efforts to an astonishing degree. His highly unorthodox writing career was not denied him. Indeed, his first abbot, Frederic Dunne, did more to encourage the writing and even the controversial autobiography than one would have thought possible in a rather rigid, pre-conciliar Cistercian monastery. Merton's superiors were wise to have allowed this writing career to flourish. It gave Merton a vocation, the abbey a mission, Trappist life a dimension it would not have had without his many books and articles.

Fidelity and consistency with self were constant concerns of Thomas Merton. His abbots speak frequently of his obedience. There was something childlike about the man. The obedience, I believe, emerged from a level of his life deeper than conformity to a vow or institutional regularity. His obedience was motivated by the fear of himself he experienced. He realized that, unchecked, he would dissipate his life.

He feared, furthermore, that he could become unfaithful to his talent as a writer and to the contemplative vocation that emerged from the writing. His obedience to the structure and substantive style of Trappist life was absolutely necessary for the preservation of his personal integrity. The silence of the Trappist life helped to tame his overwrought personality. It also worked to restrain some of his writing excesses. In their own way, even the censors helped.

Writing: A Career and a Vocation

There is a period in his writing, especially in the 1960s, when Merton's work is no longer curtailed by the limits of pre-conciliar Catholic theology. Nor is it checked by censors who sometimes disagree outright but at other times force more careful revisions. At this time, in his book, *Seeds of Destruction,* he makes wild statements about white Americans ready to burn blacks in crematoria. He attacks white liberals mercilessly and finds blacks blameless in every situation.

Those who read Merton long enough learn not to take his more extreme positions seriously. He balances his thinking eventually. He is always saved by his own humor with his own foibles and by his capacity to change positions easily when change seems to be in order. His temperament led him to act abruptly in defense of a cause; his previous experience prompted him to anger against oppression. Sometimes the abruptness and the anger led to reckless rhetoric and fundamental contradiction.

The virtues far outnumbered the defects. Merton could not command so large and diversified an audience for so long a time unless he possessed an uncommon talent. His range was simply breathtaking. He wrote about civil rights and peace, spiritual direction and Scripture, world literature and Asian philosophy. He wrote poetry and biography, history and fiction, autobiography and essays. He edited books and translated poetry. He analyzed thinkers from the pre-Christian era, early Christianity, the Middle Ages, and modern times. He wrote of Mahatma Gandhi and Chuang Tzu, of Cistercian saints and desert mystics, of Bernard of Clairvaux and Albert Camus. He wrote journals and book reviews, drama and theology, anthropology and sermons.

More than all else he wanted to make his mark as a poet. His poetry included not only formal verse but at times the medium of prose poetry, which he used more effectively. The closing section of *The Sign of Jonas,* entitled "Fire Watch, July 4, 1952," is a prose passage of uncommon beauty, rich in symbols and metaphors, resonant with themes of pilgrimage and journey. The author takes his turn on a fire watch through the monastery late at night. As he makes his rounds, he reflects on himself, his fellow monks, the Trappist vocation, the meaning of life. The prose is incandescent and serene at one and the same time, afire with vibrancy and yet mellow with the softness of early night and the quiet of darkness.

Merton is baptized by his experience "in the rivers of night" and supported in the darkness by the fragile light he carries. He shines that light, comparing it to an alert tennis ball, on the walls of the monastery; the past and the present leap into his consciousness with an imagery as rich as life. "Little children, love one another" he reads on one wall; sentences from the liturgy, on another; near a kiln he beholds a clay Christ that came from the heart of a young monk. The light shines on the floor Merton waxed regularly when he was a postulant, on the door to the tribune where first he heard the monks sing the psalms, on the books in the library that describe Carthusian life and continue to tempt him with their song of silence and hermitage.

The night is hot almost beyond bearing. On his rounds he smells the duck and the bread of the deserted kitchen, the cotton of the tailor shop, the jungle of wet clothes in the laundry. The meditation touches the very center of his being and he begins to search, not a building, but his soul with lamps and questions in the healing darkness. He smells again the frozen straw of his first Christmas in the monastery. He was there only two weeks when he celebrated the best Christmas of his life, a Christmas in which he had nothing left in the world except God. He recalls his motives in entering the monastery, and turns and weeps with shame.

The walk through the monastery takes him higher and higher toward the belfry and the roof of the building. He looks on the place where his trembling voice uttered the vows that bound him to this community;

the place, where, later, his eager hands were anointed with oil and the priesthood. As he reaches the top of the building, the point where the majesty and strength of the edifice are most apparent, he recalls that nothing lasts. Roofs of houses cave in; walls crack and buckle; the holiest of buildings turns to ashes while watchmen in the night create theories about their permanence. Not only buildings but men decay, the power of their bodies turned to weakness in the length of their days.

It is a night of ecstasy and silence, of brilliant light and overwhelming darkness, of sounds and stillness. The night is filled with murmurs, the walls with traveling noises that rush and gibber in the distance. Finally, the door from the belfry to the roof swings open upon an endless sea of darkness that takes Merton to the moon and out among the stars, a vision reminiscent of Dante's *Purgatorio*. "Is this what death is like?" he wonders. He stands higher than the treetops and walks in the shining blackness. He is cooled by the breeze of darkness, by the sight of the frozen stars. And he prays with all his heart that he has not violated the silence by his words and books, by the fame he has brought the monastery, by the unworthiness of his presence. It is a tender night, a moment of darkness that sheds light on the heart of a hermit, radiance into the spirit of a mystic. He remembers that God hears his cries even before they are uttered, that God sleeps in his breast and offers in the silence mercy after mercy, forgiveness without end. A dove begins a hushed flight from the stirring leaves. Merton sees now not only the darkness but also the dew. It is morning; the night watch is over; a new fire stirs the earth, not one to be feared because it will take away the peaceful night but a source of light in the heavens giving birth to another day.

There are passages in *Seeds of Contemplation* that also qualify as poetry. The final two chapters, "*Contemplata Tradere*" and "Pure Love," are also reminiscent of Dante. There is a purity about them, a suffusion of light, a contemplative sensitivity, a profound, poetic, moving quality. Throughout the book there are captivating images and unusual, almost metaphysical conceits.

Merton describes the mystery of God by comparing himself to a word uttered by God containing a thought generated by the heart and mind of God. No word comprehends the voice that utters it. Contemplation is described as a country whose center is everywhere and whose circumference is nowhere. One journeys in such a land not by motion but by immobility, not by walking but by standing still. The restlessness of the human mind and the passion of the human heart for affluence are compared to crows. We collect everything that glitters even though our nests become cluttered and uncomfortable with the useless metal in them.

There are insightful passages about writing and poetry. A writer, Merton warns, must never be so cautious that the writing cannot be criticized. To elude negative criticism is to write material not worth reading.

In a comparison between poetry and contemplation, Merton observes that a poet enters into the self to create poetry and a contemplative enters into an awareness of God to create silence and prayer. A religious poet must first be not religious, but a poet.

Acquisitiveness is not limited to material possessions. Some people collect recollections rather than cars, crave interior peace as though it were a bottle of wine, seek the presence of God with the same thirst they might have for a glass of beer. The need to possess is so pervasive that we often collect spiritual things that clutter our lives after material things have been set aside.

Seeds of Contemplation and *The Sign of Jonas* come from deep within the psyche of Merton. They are the perfect medium for his poetic talent. They are also lyrical celebrations of his contemplative life. Lyrics are the gift of the young; elder poets seldom compose them. Merton is young in years and young in his vocation as he sings of joy and freedom. Faith makes him a poet; poetry makes him a contemplative; contemplation makes him a mystic.

The novel *My Argument with the Gestapo* also qualifies as prose poetry, but the atmosphere is troubled rather than serene. The novel is filled with the tension of Merton's final years before entering the monastery. It reflects the cynicism he felt about the world and himself, the uncertainty he experienced about his life and his destiny. The novel is a surrealistic excursion into a world adazzle with the magic of Joycean language and with the medium of what will later be called anti-poetry.

The first six volumes of Merton's poetry are akin to the prose poetry of *Seeds of Contemplation* and *The Sign of Jonas.* They are poems, for the most part, of happiness, serenity, and meditation. On occasion there is anger but the rage and confusion are, on the whole, muted. The last two volumes of Merton's poetry, *Cables to the Ace* and *The Geography of Lograire,* are in the same vein as *My Argument with the Gestapo.*

The connections in the career of Merton are constant. *My Argument with the Gestapo* (written in 1941) is a preparation for *The Geography of Lograire* (written in 1968), which follows twenty-seven years later. The novel is written the year Merton enters the monastery; the epic poem is composed in the year of his death.

The novel and epic are anti-poems of sorts. Both are autobiographical; both are concerned with the decay of civilization. In both the author is on a journey; in the novel, on foot or by car; in the epic, circling the globe by jet and freighter, ice-breaker and riverboat, cargo plane and pack animal. In neither the novel nor the epic does the author find home. In both, the passion for nonviolence is intense.

The effectiveness Merton had in the blending of prose and poetry accounts for the success of his final poems, *Cables to the Ace* and *The Geography of Lograire.* These are not prose poems as much as poems written with a considerable dependence on prose. In any case, they are good, they work; they enchant and mystify, challenge and assuage.

The admixture of prose and poetry in his writing conspires to give us in the journals some of Merton's best work. The journal entries are episodic as poetry tends to be, concentrated in their intensity, suggestive rather than fully declarative. *The Secular Journal* is rich in sounds; *The Sign of Jonas* is powerful in its silence; *Conjectures of a Guilty Bystander* aches with the longing for human connections; *The Asian Journal* is tense with creative effort; *A Vow of Conversation* is unforgettable in its visual imagery, its rituals at the hermitage, its compatibility with the rhythms of nature. Seven volumes of his journals will be published after his death and five volumes of his letters. They do not, however, achieve the poetic resonance of the journals written with the intention of publishing them.

The proclivity for prose and poetry explains why his systematic writing is singularly poor. His forte was the spontaneous, intuitive insight, the awareness of a reality without the consideration of logic or contradiction. He was not an encyclopedist; he was an essayist. The prose poetry accounts also for the success of *The Seven Storey Mountain.* The autobiography is an excursion into a world of vivid experiences, lyrical encounters with life, mystical yearning. It is less the narrative of a life than the story of a soul or the song of a poet or the symbol of an age. Its model is Dante and the intrepid journey to the light in the *Divina Commedia.* Its title comes, as we know, from Dante.

The Seven Storey Mountain is Odysseus in a new key, longing for home, standing at the end, in wonder and gratitude, on the shore of

Ithaca. It is thematically close to Milton as Milton desires, loses, and gains paradise. Eden is recovered in Gethsemani; paradise is not now a free gift but the fruit of suffering and death. The most vivid passages in the autobiography are those of childhood, Edenic memories, the lost innocence of youth. The opening pages are complemented by the closing chapters built around purity and liturgical chant as Eden returns and Gethsemani becomes, not a bitter night of agony beneath a bleak tree, but a garden of paradise and peace.

The poetry in him sparkles in the translation he does in the work of Chuang Tzu, a fourth-century B.C.E. Chinese philosopher who is considered the authentic spokesman for Taoism. The form is prose, but the language is under so much pressure and is so paradoxical that it approaches poetry. The book is built around the complementarity of opposites rather than their contradiction, an approach that would match Merton's thought and writing. *The Wisdom of the Desert Fathers* is another example of the medium in which Merton excelled. The humor and brevity allow Merton to show his skill as translator and his capacity for poetic terseness.

Poetry is probably the most striking when it develops organically rather than logically. Poetry is not a cerebral but a holistic response to reality. A good poem holds together because it belongs together rather than because there is a reasoned consistency to it. This organic quality of writing is most typical of Merton's prose. There is no system, no conceptual model, no thematic continuity to link his many works. Indeed, they seem dull and devitalized when they are reduced to categories and catalogs. Merton's prose lives; it is not constructed. It develops not only from chapter to chapter but from book to book. The growth is developmental but not designed. At the end of the process, when the career is over, one can see what has happened. Individual parts are often weak, as they are in any organism. Certain books retard the process or contradict its forward movement. But on the whole the élan vital works its way.

The reader arrives at *Zen and the Birds of Appetite* and the consummation of *The Geography of Lograire,* but does not know quite how he or she has gotten there. The passage from *The Ascent to Truth* to *Conjectures of a Guilty Bystander,* or from *What Are These Wounds?* to *Contemplation in a World of Action,* is a passage the mind can neither fathom nor follow. It is a life passage, an organic reality, cognitively baffling, existentially comprehensible.

The organic model serves not only to connect book to book in the long Merton canon, but also to unite the writing to the writer. Merton writes out of his life experience; his writing leads back to his life for its proper interpretation. The correlation between the man and his work is not a luxury in the study of Merton, but an indispensable element in the process. The writing grows out of a dramatic life, a symbolic and archetypal journey, personal experiences that illumine the man, his work, and the century in which he lived. Even his death in the East serves as a symbol to clarify his writings on the East.

When one considers the corpus of Merton's work, one realizes that it was not a rigid schedule that enabled him to write so much as a psychic drive. Those who knew Merton well would never describe him as rigid in his schedule or task-oriented in his approach to life. He is described most often as someone full of life and life's energy. This fullness finds expression in manuscript after manuscript as the writing becomes a way of breathing, a source of nourishment, and the stuff of personal survival. In the written word he finds silence; in silence, a need to write again. Some of his friends were mistaken—indeed, Zilboorg was mistaken—when they saw the writing as a violation of Cistercian silence. His Cistercian vocation, his contemplative calling, would have faltered and failed had he not written. Even had he remained physically in the monastery his life would have been diminished spiritually without his books.

He does not write history as history but history as cultural critique. History for him is a developmental process that explains something more profound, namely, the life out of which it is made. When he writes another inferior book, *The Waters of Siloe,* there are virtues because the history of Cistercians in America is approached in a way more creative than the material might suggest. The first Trappists who came to the United States sail on the *Brunswick* with other idealistic passengers who travel to create a utopian community in the New World. Merton always enlarges the scope of his vision, The year is 1848; the community members call themselves Icarians.

This touch of "secular" history is rich in symbolism and meaning. The Trappists also come to build a utopian community. Their community will last longer, although its utopian character will be threatened by its very success, by the rigidity and institutionalism that easily stifle the spirit. The Trappist community will have a capacity for self-renewal and reform, however, which the short-lived Icarian group did not possess.

The utopian connection is rich in meaning, because the first Trappists sail to a country in the grip of idealism. They arrive at midpoint in a century that gives the United States Ralph Waldo Emerson and Henry David Thoreau. The same century will witness utopian communities at Oneida, Brook Farm, Fruitlands, New Harmony, Amana. Cistercian history is developed by Merton in the life context of the forces and influences that shape both the century and the Trappist community. Later, Merton will become a reformer who brings his own century to bear on the character of Cistercian life.

As *The Waters of Siloe* progresses, one is reminded throughout not only of the Trappists whose history is the main focus, but also of the cultural background against which this occurs. One hears not only the bells of Gethsemani, but the cannons of the American Civil War; not only the chant of the Roman liturgy but the trumpets of Nazi Germany and Fascist Italy; not only the farm machinery of the silent monks but the roar of the atomic bomb.

This organic and dialectical approach is present in biography as well as in history. Merton's life of Bernard of Clairvaux, *The Last of the Fathers,* is not effective as biography but is creative in its methodology. He gives us the history of the saint by selecting a limited number of themes or incidents in the life of Bernard that typify him. No effort is made to be comprehensive. The method works. We do not gather much data from the biography, but we are given insights that transcend data and interpret the man. He was too great, Merton observes, to be captured in his entirety. Merton considers only moments in the life of Bernard: the young abbot; the midpoint of his life; the high point of his influence when he is, practically speaking, papal in his impact on the Church.

Merton observes that Bernard contained the entire twelfth century in himself. The observation describes well Merton's career in the twentieth century. The connections between the two extend beyond this comparison. Abbot Flavian Burns believes that Merton is one of the greatest Trappists since Bernard and capable of being considered together with him.[17] Merton equates the many failures of Bernard with his successes in the construction of a significant life. The equation applies with equal force to Merton. One of the neglected characteristics of Merton's holiness and genius is his willingness to attempt new things, to fail, and to call attention to the failure. The journals of Merton are replete with such material. He is candid also in declaring his lack of talent for the office of abbot and in the self-critique of his books that he offers.

Merton cites in *The Last of the Fathers* an ingenious principle for discerning genuine spirituality from its counterfeits. Spiritual renewal is real when it affects every level of life around it. It is artificial when it withdraws people from the way life functions for most of the human race. Spiritual experience fosters human development; it does not degenerate into fanaticism or elitism.

Spirituality, like writing, is organic in its development. A spiritual life is effective if it is rooted in culture and nourishes what is best in that culture. Spirituality flows from life to life. It multiplies itself, as biological life does, by human contact. It conducts a dialogue with the world, a dialectical conversation in which it gains and loses, gives and takes. The year Merton writes *The Last of the Fathers* is 1954; it is not one of his better works. The turbulent changes soon to influence him as he turns to social protest, Zen Buddhism, and anti-poetry are foreshadowed in this work, especially in his insistence that spirituality has a mission to its own moment in history.

The volume on Clairvaux is an insight into Merton. He presents Bernard as a man of contradictions, some of which prove disastrous but many of which lead to creativity. One of the less fortunate contradictions is evident in Bernard's capacity to preach a war at the same time he develops sermons on the Canticle of Canticles. Bernard's idea of a war against Islam, the Second Crusade, was mystical in its intent, but in its fierceness, it required violent means for its accomplishment. In spite of such dreadful false starts, Bernard inspires his century and subsequent ages. Dante celebrates Bernard in paradise as the greatest of the contemplatives. Luther believed Bernard surpassed all the doctors of the Church; Calvin equated the language of Bernard with truth itself.

Writing: The Deeper Dimension

Merton's writing should not be considered solely in terms of its positive or negative characteristics. The writing reflects a more profound life operating beneath its surface.

Writing, for example, became for Merton an indispensable ingredient in the development of nonviolence. He believes that violence is akin to wordlessness. Wordlessness is not the same as violence. Wordlessness comes from a deficiency of communication; silence emerges from its accomplishment. Silence, contemplation, and nonviolence are kindred experiences. Wordlessness, activism, and violence reinforce one another. A society bent on violence restricts the use of meaningful words. In its place it uses verbiage and inarticulate noise to arrest thought. Such empty words defeat meaning in every engagement.

For Merton, writing had a unique power to engender nonviolence by leading people to thought, to silence, to creative communication. By writing, Merton practiced pacifism; the practice led to further writing. Without articulation, the anarchistic tendencies in Merton might have borne the bitter fruit of violence. There were unresolved angers in him; he knew the hunger of deprived affection; he resented the oppressors of others with a personal and visceral reaction.

The writing helped in other ways. It became a means by which he learned to touch other people. The writing entered into the kind of contemplation he sought, which embraced the world as it encountered God.

> The human affections do not receive much gratification in a life of silence and solitude. The almost total lack of self-expression, the frequent inability to "do things for" other people in a visible and tangible way can sometimes be a torture and lead to great frustration.[18]

From this point forward he begins to think of himself as a writer. The sense of self-integrity that good writing requires is now more explicitly formulated. His writing becomes more prolific as his words make his spirit of love incarnate. The writing converts him into a commitment to social justice, and into an encounter with the sacred in the midst of secular experience.

The writing leads to sacrifice of self in his effort to achieve purity of heart. He notes that "some of the most virtuous men in the world are also the bitterest and most unhappy, because they have unconsciously come to believe that all their happiness depends on their being more virtuous than other men."[19] "Virtue," therefore, becomes a source if alienation and eventually an excuse for violence. He sees his own role in a different light: "I will never be able to find myself if I isolate myself from the rest of mankind as if I were a different kind of being."[20] He begins, therefore, to write journals whose candor causes conflicts and whose self-disclosure makes some of his friends uneasy. He feels compelled, however, to show that mystics and contemplatives walk the same path and experience the same missteps as others. He is not a different kind of being. Writing will make this clear to others, perhaps give them courage and even hope so that they will not despair of their lives.

The dynamo that will energize his life will be honesty and self-integrity:

> Many poets are not poets for the same reason that many religious are not saints: they never succeed in being themselves.... They wear out their minds and bodies in a hopeless endeavor to have someone else's experiences....[21]

Merton writes these words early in his career as a writer and applies them to his prose. It takes him longer as a poet to find his own voice. Eventually he does. But it is a poetic voice one does not expect to hear from someone in formal religious life, indeed from a Cistercian, a mystic, and a hermit. It is, however, the voice of a brother, a thoroughly human voice, the voice of one who has felt the pain and the glory of his own times. His poetry turns to the secular world for its theme, to anti-poetry for its form, to an analysis of his own psyche and the psyche of the age. His sanctity also takes an original turn. He identifies with others, especially those disregarded by the official Church. He writes favorably of atheists and black militants, of pacifists and Catholic liberals. He believes that clerical celibacy should be optional, authority structures less rigid, monastic life more diverse and resilient.

Toward the end of his life he observes:

> There can be no question that the great crisis in the Church today is the crisis of authority brought on by the fact that the Church, as an institution and organization, has in fact usurped the place of the Church as a community of persons united in love and in Christ.... Love is equated with obedience and conformity within the framework of an impersonal corporation. The Church is preached as a communion, but is run in fact as a collectivity, and even as a totalitarian collectivity.[22]

He tries to write and pray in his own language, from his own experience. His uniqueness is the foundation of his spiritual nobility and of his artistic genius. A fellow monk, Basil Pennington, has written well of Merton in this regard:

> Genius is rare, holiness even rarer, but when they make their appearance as they unquestionably did in Merton, they have the power to pass beyond the last frontier; death itself can make no claim on them.[23]

The writing and the prayer helped Merton overcome the shame of being human. It conquered the fear that our personal fallibilities, if acknowledged, would take away our dreams and visions. Writing made him comfortable with who he was; contemplation deepened and sharpened the awareness. He became sensitive to the simple rhythms and rituals of everyday life. In his hermitage, near the end of his life, he writes of the music of the rain and the sound of fire, the freedom of the clouds and the impetuosity of the wind. He writes of the smell of coffee and the feel of water, of the enveloping darkness and the tranquil intrusion of deer, of the distant bells of Gethsemani. He heard them once at St. Bonaventure in New York and traveled home to this abbey. He hears them now in his hermitage and they stir in him vague memories and unfulfilled yearning, hopes that were never realized, and joys he had not anticipated. He is now a Catholic who has learned the poverty of the Gospel and the simplicity of Zen. He is himself a Christian paradox whose simplicity appears complex to those who have their own image of what a monk must be. He is a Zen koan whose resolution into clarity is unattainable, especially to those whose religious categories are tired and prosaic. He is himself. His writing says as much and his life reinforces the declaration.

Merton's friend and biographer, John Howard Griffin, traces Merton's appeal to the time for which he wrote and to the personal force behind the writing:

> Merton's writings coincided with a period in history—the years following World War II—when many were confused, bewildered, and searching for something more than religious platitudes. Also, Merton's extraordinary personality permeated his works.[24]

Merton's closest friend and confidant, Robert Lax, saw the interconnections in Merton's life more clearly than most: "the poems help the calligraphies, the calligraphies help the poems; the poems and the calligraphies help the manifestos; you will see, you will see."[25]

The antinomies became interconnection because of the writing. Writing was, as we have said, his fundamental calling. He writes in *Conjectures of a Guilty Bystander* that he has a sense death is near although he is only forty-seven. Merton does indeed die some six years later. In the light of this thought he reflects on the chief concern of his life: writing. He is regretful that it has taken so much energy from him, but he realizes also that without writing he would have become too heavy a burden for himself.

In the earlier years, he had struggled with monasticism and whether it should be more important in his life than writing. The intensity of the dilemma is especially evident in *The Seven Storey Mountain* and *The Sign of Jonas.* He speaks of the problem in terms of life and death. He does not exaggerate. His identity and his integrity depend upon writing. As he begins to publish more regularly, he becomes more peaceful. The shrill tone mellows. His fears subside. Merton accepts monasticism and writing as complementary vocations. He eventually recognized explicitly what was unconsciously sensed many years earlier. His commitment to writing was even more passionate than his commitment to monasticism. It is not as though the two vocations were exclusive. Indeed, each depended upon the other for its development. It was a matter of simple preference or, perhaps, a question of greater need. He had to write; he chose to be a monk. He wrote seriously for as long as he could remember; he was a monk for only half of his life.

> It is possible to doubt whether I have become a monk (a doubt I have to live with), but it is not possible to doubt that I am a

> writer, that I was born one and will most probably die as one... it is...my vocation.[26]

The writing, especially in his journals, leads him to some of the most crucial decisions in his life. *The Secular Journal* settles for him the question about whether he should enter the monastery. *The Sign of Jonas* resolves his problem about the compatibility of a career as a writer and a Trappist vocation. *Conjectures of a Guilty Bystander* moves him into the radical social commitments of the last decade of his life. In *The Asian Journal,* he becomes convinced that Asian religions and cultures are not only genuine in themselves but indispensable to Christianity and the West.

Through his years of monastic life, when issues of identity will be posed again and again for Merton, writing becomes the sure point, the lodestar, the faithful and dependable experience. In the writing he is made whole and his world takes shape in a manner that allows him to make commitments to it.

Writing not only gives but takes. It wears him out and disgusts him. In *A Vow of Conversation,* he complains of nausea because of his excessive work. He is sick constantly. The same month that he complains of his dissatisfaction with himself and his writing, he suffers from colitis and severe pain from a spinal disc. The back pain becomes severe that spring. He worries about cancer: Both parents had died of cancer; he is a candidate.

Merton is afflicted also with nervous exhaustion. The most dramatic instance of this is the year and a half after his ordination. He is incapable of writing during that time. Merton is ordained in 1949; *The Seven Storey Mountain* had been published the previous summer; the strain of trying to decide whether he could publish and remain a Trappist is intense.

Throughout 1964 and 1965 Merton suffers stress-related ailments and emotional tension. In August the skin starts to peel from his hands and he needs gloves to type. By August of the following year, he will wonder about marriage and remember Jinny Burton. At the same time he will be tested for ulcers. It is a bad year.

The doubts about the writing and the recurrence of physical problems unsettle him. He also questions celibacy and monasticism. He reasons, however, that the distress makes his writing more real. His appeal to others depends, he believes, upon the fact that "I'm not sure of myself." He consoles himself with the thought that perhaps all talented people are inconsistent. But the writing now seems a burden. Therefore everything appears unbearable.

This is also the time when the personal conflicts between Merton and Abbot James Fox are at their height. He lashes out in anger and pain. Obedience seems to be little more than submission to the prejudices and fetishes of another. In January of 1964 he complains of being used, exploited, cheated by the monastery. In the same month, he is disturbed by Cardinal Francis Spellman, who apparently rejected a film script Merton had written for the Vatican pavilion at the New York World's Fair. Spellman, according to Merton, wanted a text less ecumenical, one subtly manipulative, capable of proselytizing without appearing to do so overtly.

Two months later, Rome silences him on the issue of nuclear war. He becomes critical of a Church that imperiously imposes its power on defenseless monks whom it controls and yet cowers before Nazism in one generation and repressive Latin American regimes in the next. It is a bad year. He always feared the writing might jeopardize his vocation as a monk and a contemplative. Now he is silenced, not by choice or because of a monastic rule, but because he is thought to be dangerous.

There are powers in the Church that favor nuclear arsenals, massive armies, military dictatorships. These are judged less dangerous than Merton's words. He is near despair. Perhaps all his efforts, all his writing, have been useless. If he loses faith in the writing, in the poetry and in the books, in the protest and in the journals, he will falter as a person. He presses on and writes his heart out in his journals. Unusual dreams disturb him at night. A woman who speaks Latin approaches and flees from Merton with her dress torn. Is she the symbol of a Church that is lacerated from its own defects? Or is she a symbol of violence, or sexual desire? Merton is sick with the thought of his falseness, crushed by the fact that the meaning of his life and calling is so elusive despite the many books and endless words.

He writes movingly of Cardinal John Henry Newman at this time, of the man's religious profundity. Yes, there are good people in the Church. He admires Newman especially for sustaining the admixture of nonsense and persecution he suffered at the hands of the hierarchy.

The dreams continue. Some of them are more gentle. He dreams of a mother's love and of his own childhood, of the happy times in France and of Asia as a place he would love to visit. He experiences a need for compassion, gentleness, understanding.

Images of death crowd him. Worse than death is the fear that because of all this the writing might not go right.

He tries to get it all down on paper. He is careful to record all the defects. He does not want to be a Catholic icon. He will not allow others to honor him as a mystic until they have seen him as a man. He is impatient with people who believe contemplatives are free from envy or sexual temptation or anger. Even hermits fall in love. And he does. She is a nurse. It is summer (1966). He is troubled. He writes some of his best poetry about the relationship. It is sexually charged, tender, heartbreaking, impossible, and unforgettable.[27] It ends. And he dies soon after.

His poetry now becomes more intimate and personal. He writes his long anti-poems; his great autobiographical epic is begun. He is back to the beginning as the end approaches. *The Seven Storey Mountain* is repeated, but this time in verse and with another name, *The Geography of Lograire.* Love conquers now not only the God he sought in passion through his vocation and vows but the world he wept for in secret and longing. Out of the crucible of conflict and contradiction a contemplative is born whose spirit is marked by compassion.

As the end approaches, he journeys to New York and touches base with it before he dies. Here the writing began and here he was baptized. Here he met his lifelong friends Mark Van Doren and Dan Walsh, Bob Lax and Ed Rice.

Reality cannot be encountered if he repeats the past. He must go one step further on the journey into the future. New York City becomes for him a catalyst for the memories he must not lose and for the hopes that stir him restlessly.

In his early work, he had spoken of the "water of bitterness and contradiction." But more tranquil journeys would have destroyed him. He had to live close to the dividing line between homecoming and alienation, between life and death, compliance and disobedience, poetry and prose, East and West, the world and the Church, rules of silence and vows of conversation.

There were no limits when he was writing: books, readers, ideas seemed endless. The exile he feared was not exclusion from the community of his fellow monks. He seldom speaks of community on this level. Nor did he fear exclusion from the Church's approval. The exile he feared was exclusion from writing. He was most deeply disturbed in his life when people put restraints on his writing, when Cardinal Spellman refused to allow his work to be made public, when Rome prohibited his books on peace.

Thus, it is not too much to claim, as Merton does, in a letter to Jacques Maritain, the French philosopher, that for him sanctity is "connected with books and with writing." "If I were forbidden to write." he confesses on another occasion, "I would soon land in a mental hospital."

> For the writer who does not write, all his life is a slow form of poison; and every good writer knows this, and every writer who is afraid of spiritual corruption must, finally, come back to writing.[28]

Life, for Merton, is a literary quest, It is also a mystic search for the ultimate Word. Paradoxically, such a journey requires profound silence. Writing is a vow of conversation rooted in silence. A writer who does not listen well never knows what to say. One enters the silence not to be alone but to learn how to speak.

At the conclusion of *A Vow of Conversation,* it is September. Merton is now in the hermitage, watching shy deer approach, sensing their softness, longing to touch them. The deer are a symbol of people whom he often viewed from too great a distance. He longed to touch others and feared the encounter. By writing, he kept the longing alive; through words, he kept people near him. One day perhaps the shyness and hesitation would pass. Then he would no longer fear the limitation that love of others brings, the immobility marked by every embrace. One day he would hold on to others and experience not enclosure but freedom.

CHAPTER THREE

The Measure of Human Pain

Pain is part of the process. Everyone learns this. From the shedding of blood that initiates birth to the last gasp of astonishment in the face of death, we are encircled in suffering. The biography of a human being is also a history of anguish. The way one reacts to the suffering of life matters more, in creative and human terms, than the suffering itself. We become the people we are through the disadvantages and conflicts we prefer to more comfortable alternatives.

A record of the life of Thomas Merton is also a record of the conflicts and contradictions. Our interest in him in this chapter has something to do with the creative tensions he generates and sustains.

When matters are too ordered in his life, Thomas Merton becomes uncreative. By the time he reaches the 1950s, his writing becomes stale. The turbulence of his life before conversion, the tensions and anxieties of his early monastic years, the preparation for priesthood, the problems involved in deciding whether he should be a writer or not, are now behind him. Books like *No Man Is an Island* show the uncreative tranquility of it all. He knows too much, has too many answers, because he sees only one angle of life. If something else had not happened in his life, his vocation as a writer, even his identity as a person, certainly his monastic calling, would have been jeopardized. Conflict energizes him; resolution undoes him. Again, the paradox. The man who sought peace in the Abbey of Gethsemani was happy as long as his vocation gave him little peace. Peace of soul and tranquility of life are not the same thing. It is possible to be turbulent and still at one and the same moment.

Merton is most shallow when the dialectic in his life is not sharp enough. As we have said, something else had to occur or the serenity would have destroyed him. The something else is an avalanche of new ideas and experiences. He ventures outside the monastery and realizes at the same conference at St. John's University, Collegeville, Minnesota, where he had the painful encounter with Dr. Gregory Zilboorg, that God can be met deeply outside Gethsemani. This was the first trip of any consequence he had made outside the abbey since his entrance into it in 1941.

The year is 1956. As a result of this experience, the need to make the world a monastery diminishes in his work. His involvement with secular concerns intensifies. The secular is to be not only changed but encountered. It has its own revelation, its own spiritual character, its own sacramentality. It must. The vast majority of human beings give most or all of their lives to the secular. If there is no sacred character to the secular, the sacred is an insignificant experience for practically everyone.

Further ideas and experiences help to alter his course. The fascination with the East develops. The road he now travels is not only a Western road. He seeks an Eastern summit and the light of new approaches to life and monasticism. In the East, he is reborn, not without reference to his Western existence or to his Christian roots. He is reborn in the East and he dies there.

In the West there is a new event. The Second Vatican Council occurs. Western thinking is radically opened to new forms. Merton is saved by a Western council, an Eastern journey, and a secular commitment. His writing improves. He becomes more critical in his theology and, paradoxically, less critical of people and the way they live. His poetry goes in different directions. Some of the poetry fails, but the failure is more noteworthy than some of his former successes. He enters the last decade of his life, his most creative years. He moves away from books like *No Man Is an Island* and speaks of how insular he has been.

In the twenty years from *The Seven Storey Mountain* to *The Geography of Lograire* he is changed profoundly. *The Seven Storey Mountain* succeeded because it put the secular and the sacred side by side. It failed because one superseded the other. The book is narrow, the author is arrogant. Merton had the right ingredients, but he dealt with them artificially and lost his balance. He overpowered the secular with the sacred. In *The Geography of Lograire* the secular and the sacred exist together and with equal force. The sacred emerges from the secular and does not eliminate it. The tensions are kept alive, wedded rather than resolved, not marred but married.

He worries about the Church, its ideology and politics, the people given power in the structure, their awful need to be right. He is frightened and fascinated by Catholicism. All sanctity is born in conflict. He knows this. The answer is to embrace and reject at the same time. He cannot divorce himself from Catholicism. He really does not want that. Life with the Church may be at times a sad affair. But it becomes tragic only if one accepts Catholicism blindly, he reasons. And so he will be discerning. He will pick and choose. He will be selective, not to be arbitrary or self-indulgent, but to prohibit others from being autocratic. He will decide, not to be rebellious, but to be himself. He must not pass into the hands of another, especially into the hands of those intent on doing good. They often do the most harm. He must allow the tradition to touch him but not with so great a hold that creativity is stifled. He will be committed; he will not be beholden. The Church is a paradoxical reality. It easily forgets that it has no right to hold on, since its purpose is to pass away. Its people are to pass over into the keeping of a deeper Love. A deeper Love. That was it. A Love that does not die. A mother dies. And a father dies. And John Paul dies—all too soon. The Love he needs is more than father or mother, more than brother.

Although it is fallible more often than it admits, the Church pretends to be infallible. This infallibility business will destroy it. Infallibility is too easy. It reduces the tensions. It tries to hold the truth in a formula or keep people in its power. Infallibility passes too easily into politics in the Church. The combination of infallibility and politics will bring about a crisis of order in the Church. Infallibility and mandatory celibacy may destroy the Church as an influence in the world. The Church cannot continue its mission successfully unless its administrators are ready to make more drastic changes in it than they seem capable of doing.

Merton explores these ideas in *Conjectures of a Guilty Bystander.* The temptation of the Church is not deserting Christ but possessing him. Ecclesial infidelity is not a question of an affair with another god but trying to control God so thoroughly that God cannot be real for anyone beyond the Church. At the heart of the Church there abides not only love but a tyrannical spirit.

The Church is more effective in its need than in its infallibility, more evangelical in its shortcomings than in its security. "Life without problems is hopeless," he writes in *No Man Is an Island.* In fallibility, there is salvation. Infallibility, after all, is not a human experience. A Church that may die is cherished more ardently than one whose indestructibility has no need of us. Infallibility and indestructibility draw the focal point of our attention to the structure and the institution. But it is necessary to transcend the Church in order to encounter God.

The need we have for the Church has something to do with its own need. Its need for God and for us is the heart of its identity and mission.

Dialectics and Dynamics

Merton was intrigued with the play of dialectics, contradictions, paradox. He found abundant evidence everywhere, from ancient Greek to early Chinese thinkers and Christian writers. His discovery of such dynamic approaches was due not only to the fact that they were there but to his own need to find them. He was not a logical thinker in the classic sense of the word.

The attention he gave to the thought of Herakleitos is to the point. The world Herakleitos lived in was a world dominated by Homer, the Olympian gods, laws of mechanical necessity, and a preference for static and changeless order. In such a world, Herakleitos spoke on behalf of the mysterious, ambivalent, elusive quality of existence. He found an attentive disciple in Merton.

Herakleitos believed that fire was the primary element in the universe. Modern science would not, of course, accept this. But Merton sees the Herakleitean emphasis on fire as an image or symbol of something more profound. Fire was Herakleitos's way of preferring a process or evolutive view of reality to one that was static. In a synthesis that brings the thought of Herakleitos through the centuries and into the context of Merton's own approach, Merton observes:

> the logic of Herakleitos [i.e. harmony-in-conflict] seems to have much in common with the Tao of Lao-Tse as well as with the Word of St. John...he can say that opposites can be, from a certain point of view, the same...[that there is a] deep underlying connection of opposites....[29]

Merton saw the inevitable dialectic not only in Hellenic thought but also at the heart of Christian thinking. In the cross, he believed, "we encounter the full Christian expression of the dialectic of fullness and emptiness, *todo y nada,* void and infinity which appears at the heart of all the great traditional forms of contemplative wisdom."[30] His intent was, therefore, to bring together apparently disparate elements in an effort to reflect reality more comprehensively.

In a sense, even God, in traditional Christian language, is conceived of in terms of polarities and opposites. The Son is the opposite of the Father though united in a manner that allows paternity and filiation to occur. The identity of the two is established by their capacity to remain distinct. Indeed, the Incarnation is premised on the same model. The human is the opposite of the divine, though unity on a deeper level allows christology to be developed by a capacity of the human and the divine to remain distinct and not distant.

The dialectical tendency in Merton's thinking was not limited to abstraction or speculation. His dialectics led him into the secular world and into the arena of social involvement. It also led him to dialogue with the East.

Merton began in the 1950s to explore the possibility of forging links between the monastery and megapolis. *No Man Is an Island* shows a growing concern with the world beyond the abbey. He senses his unity with the entire human family in a scene powerfully and beautifully described in his journal, *Conjectures of a Guilty Bystander.*

> In Louisville, at the corner of Fourth and Walnut, in the center of the shopping district, I was suddenly overwhelmed with the realization that I loved all those people, that they were mine and I theirs, that we could not be alien to one another even though we were total strangers.... This sense of liberation from the illusory difference was such a relief and such a joy to me that I almost laughed out loud.... Thank God, thank God that I am like other men, that I am only a man among others.[31]

Merton wanted the tensions and the opposites somehow to meet in himself. It did not matter if they were resolved there. What mattered was whether they could converge. In this he was a symbol for the twentieth century and its interest in bringing apparently impossible combinations together. The interest in the intersection of feminine and masculine characteristics, secular and sacred, East and West, objective and subjective, provides some instances of this ongoing concern.

> If I can unite in myself the thought and devotion of Eastern and Western Christendom, the Greek and the Latin Fathers, the Russians with the Spanish mystics, I can prepare in myself the reunion of divided Christians.... We must contain all divided worlds in ourselves.[32]

For Merton, paradox and contrast were the essence of life. He wanted a blurring of lines to occur so that realities passed easily into their opposites. His approach is not unlike modern physics in its search for the links between relativity and the absolute, between matter and antimatter, between unified field equations and elusive natural forces. His spirituality was built on an agony of ambivalence, a confidence that emerged not from certitude but from multiplied probability, an ecstasy born not out of discovery but from perplexity in the face of impossible alternatives. He was a hermit who sought the world as ardently as it sought him, a mystic who loved the sound of human life as much as the silence of God.

When Merton came to write of the Bible late in his career he saw it as an expression of an approach to life he and the century had come to adopt as their own. The Bible was seen as a struggle, a scandal, a system of contradictions. The Bible became the focal point for his emerging view of the universe. He sought not to explain it but to experience it.

> It should not be our aim merely to explain these contradictions away, but rather to use them as ways to enter into the strange and paradoxical world of meanings and experiences that are beyond us and yet often extremely and mysteriously relevant to us.[33]

The Bible makes sense when people perceive their lives are in disarray. It helps us overcome the problem we are to ourselves by introducing us to a deeper problem. It leads us from ignorance to an enigma, intensifying the mystery of life, intending not to solve but to overwhelm. "The Bible is a message of reconciliation and unity, but in order to awaken us to our need for unity, it brings out the contradictions within us and makes us aware of a fundamental division."[34]

The Bible, therefore, must not lead to a static form of faith in the individual believer, nor to a static ecclesiastical structure. It is "concerned with something far deeper than the establishment of a religious system." If the Bible is not seen in this light, the God supposedly preached from it is a dead God. God becomes in such a distortion not a living and loving relationship but a rigid, controlled, suffocating experience.

The search for God intensifies our contradictions. Merton writes in *Thoughts in Solitude* that contemplation helps us to live "in a silence which so reconciles the contradictions within us that, although they remain within us, they cease to be a problem."

The dialectics of Greece and of the Bible fascinate Merton. He finds evidence of the same in Asia, especially in the thought of Chuang-tzu. Chuang-tzu's thought has as its central focus the complementarity of opposites. He writes that the point of Tao is to watch "Yes" and "No" pursue their alternating course around the circumference.

The search for an authority greater than his own leads Merton back to his own conscience. His yearning for a home keeps him on the journey.

The silence of Gethsemani makes the communication with the world possible; the celebrity brought about by his own writing makes withdrawal and contemplation more urgent. Merton becomes a mystic who can easily fall in love, a lover who cannot be defined by artificial relationship, a Cistercian who finds radical new possibilities for his community by a careful study of its oldest records. His spiritual life is richest when he creates it from the materials of a profane world.

Nonviolence

Merton's involvement with nonviolence brought him into contact with one of the great movements of the century in which he lived. His criticism of war, the nuclear arms race, and the Vietnam conflict led to his silencing by Roman authorities. He was silenced for a number of reasons. Some found it incongruous that a Cistercian monk should take sides in what was viewed as politics. Merton, however, saw his vocation in the more dialectical manner that we have been describing. For him, politics was a way of being holy. He did not especially like the excesses of some politicians. But the political order, the public arena, required a strong ethical voice.

Many who viewed Merton with admiration were shocked and disappointed by his criticism of the national power structure. For some, an attack on such an institution undermined the stability of the country, if not of the world. Furthermore, a monk could not know about problems of such complexity without special training. Merton had none.

The point Merton was making about nonviolence was not wholly political in its intent. Nonviolence represented far more than cessation of armed conflict. Indeed, he wondered about the subtle belligerence of some elements in the pacifist movement.

The Catholic pacifist movement began in earnest after a quiet retreat made by its future leaders under Thomas Merton at the hermitage.

Although Merton was close to the movement, he harbored some suspicions of it. He was never able to bring himself to exclude the moral possibility of war in every instance. His pacifism was more qualified than others may have wished. He feared that some pacifists had begun the practice of praying against others. The enemy for them included not only the adversary in military conflicts but also the opponents one met in the great national debate about peace and war. Prayer and even liturgy had become weapons. Some pacifists felt a terrible need to win and to do so at almost any cost, even if it required regarding the opponent as not fully human. They wanted victory as ardently as some militarists wanted triumph in armed conflict. Such action destroyed people less brutally than violence would have done, but it sought their destruction nonetheless. Prayer, Merton argued in *Redeeming the Time*, must not be "directed against other men, but against the evil forces which divide men into warring camps."

The dialectics in Merton's thought were obvious and, to some, infuriating. He would not side easily and simply with belligerents or pacifists. He was not, however, immobilized by the dialectic. He was outspoken to the point of being silenced and harassed. But he refused to be owned or possessed by either side. His psychological fears of being totally categorized or dominated figured in his nuanced public positions. Merton frequently baffled people by moving in another direction when they had considered him to be totally in their camp.

Merton distrusted, furthermore, the potential in the peace movement for fanaticism. His reservations were terrifyingly confirmed when a young Catholic pacifist burned himself alive in front of the United Nations building in New York. Pacifism had in it the potential of rejecting not only the war but the world. He noted that the belligerent crusader for peace implicitly carries his denial of the world to the point of wishing it to be destroyed.

Yet even granting all these reservations, Merton was unmistakably a pacifist. It was the natural fruit not only of his contemplation but also of his native instincts. His mother, as we have seen, was a staunch pacifist. His father was an artist and a very gentle man. His brother was slain in war. His long interest in Mahatma Gandhi taught him that nonviolence could be both a religious way of life and a politically effective technique. Gandhi showed Merton how nonviolence could become a path to holiness.

Even before Merton was a monk he had decided that if he were drafted into the Second World War he would not bear arms. Such a position was fiercely unpopular then. The numbers of those who saw wisdom in nonviolence increased over the next twenty years. Merton would continue to make others uncomfortable with his criticisms. He tried to bring to his task sufficient humor and self-criticism to save himself from becoming an ideologue rather than a prophet.

In a powerful image, he compared our attitude toward the necessity of war with the bizarre practice of snake handling as practiced by some fundamentalist cults. The practice derives from a literal reading of the words of Jesus about the care God has for believers. Cultists stage ceremonies in which they handle poisonous snakes and allow themselves to be bitten. No antidote is permitted. It is supposed that God will allow those to survive who are favored and blessed with grace.

Snake handling and war psychosis derive from the same source, Merton argues. Life seems tedious unless there is danger. A course of action is adopted that threatens life. The threat to life enables a bored generation to feel it is alive. Furthermore, the survivors, the victors, believe themselves chosen, special, better than the vanquished and the dead, vindicated by God or by history, by genetics or by fate. Snake handling and military victory encourage judgmental attitudes toward other people. Having passed through a trial, we are supposedly superior to those who feared the snakes or the war or who lost in their encounter with either.

The philosophy of escalation is, in modern mythology, a theatrical attempt at handling a cosmic copperhead without anxiety.

In his effort to come to terms with the many facets of nonviolence, Merton began to have reservations about the just war theory of Augustine, even though his own position was derived from it. Augustine was less radical in his pacifism than some early Christian writers. He believed war was a moral choice in some instances. It is possible, Augustine argued, to fight for peace. Augustine observed, furthermore, that men will always fight and they will sometimes intend not the destruction of the other but the preservation of their own value. The world is so made that not everyone respects limits, the rights of others, human dignity. In such cases, a reluctant recourse to arms may be necessary.

Augustine based his concept of justice and his just war theory on Cicero. He distinguished between the external violence of war, which all sensible people abhor, and the internal motives that impel the soldier. If one intends peace and the preservation of a greater good, if one fights with no hate of the enemy, as a last resort and without excess, war may be moral.

Augustine's position made sense, Merton argued, in the rational order but was untenable in the real or existential order. Augustine's approach was especially problematic because it did not exclude so-called wars of mercy waged by those who considered themselves virtuous. Augustine, moreover, did not limit such wars to wars of defense but saw a moral possibility of initiating a just war. Such a philosophy of war justifies at a later date the Crusades and the Inquisitions.

Nonviolence, however, is not a struggle against the other as much as it is a contest with ourselves. Violence derives from a set of illusions about ourselves and about the world in which we live. Nonviolence does not take its origin from the violence already present in the world, a violence it resists without further violence. It begins, rather, with resistance to our own hidden fascination with fascist or totalitarian approaches to life. It is directed "against our own violence, fanaticism and greed." It begins as an act of conscience, a spiritual search, a committed way of life. The enemy is not the other but the tendency in all of us to see ourselves as the norm and the center of human behavior. Nonviolence is a contemporary and political form of contemplation, a modern mysticism that has broad social consequences.

Merton was especially sensitive to the role of nonviolence in the perilous times in which we live. The idols we worship today, unfortunately, are not the inert and perhaps essentially harmless statues of an earlier age. We worship economic structures that leave vast numbers undernourished physically, morally, and even spiritually. These structures are dynamic, Merton reminds us; they are vitalized by human decisions. We celebrate and take refuge, not in graven images, but in nuclear weapons. We render tribute to the power and the ideology which allow us to intimidate others with the use of such devices. Our idols are neither dumb nor impotent. They "live, and speak, and smile, and dance, and allure us and lead us off to kill," writes Merton in *Faith and Violence.*

American history has given life to capitalism and to nuclear militancy. It has also fostered a solution to the problems it created. Merton read American history dialectically. There has always been in America a representative pacifist tradition. It has been nourished by Quakerism; it was evident in the first great American play, *André*, written shortly after the American Revolution; it was fostered by Thoreau and the acceptance into American law of conscientious objection. The peace movement of the 1960s and the nonviolence of Martin Luther King, Jr., were latter-day manifestations of a tendency that has not been alien to the American temper. It had antecedents in the American effort to allow the opponent to voice dissent, in the American capacity to affirm one's rights without denying the rights of another, and in the tradition of civil disobedience. If belligerence has been a sad aspect of American history, restraint has been a reality at least as often.

Merton was at times a caustic critic of the American system. But he could also justify his thought with the nobler lines in the American grain. Although he was an internationalist in his thinking, the ceremony in which he accepted American citizenship moved him deeply. It contributed to the broadening of his social consciousness and to the bonds he felt with people beyond the precincts of the abbey. It also satisfied in him a psychological need for belonging and for a sense of home.

Nonviolence is frequently undermined by an unwarranted effort to want all the answers to its dilemmas in advance. It is true that nonviolence has the appearance of naïveté. Frequently, however, the possibility of nonviolence in the lives of individuals is rejected because global nonviolence seems impossible. The witness of nonviolence, professed one by one, humanizes eventually not only the self but the social structure. The difficulty in conceiving of a political and international manifestation of nonviolence should not deter people from their personal responsibility to adopt it as a procedure in their everyday lives. The emergence of entire cultures and nations committed to nonviolence depends upon the more prosaic and practical measures taken by individuals in their own right. In *Faith and Violence*, Merton insists that answers to the many questions of nonviolence can be worked out when people begin to take the issue seriously.

There was a time when democracy was deemed unworkable, when theoretical arguments about the capriciousness of human behavior and the volatile character of large populations seemed to indicate that democracy could not function in the real order. When monarchy is the only experience available, the transfer of power by free election, responsibly and orderly, seems unreliable. When authority is established by a strong central ruler, the diffusion of that authority to other groups appears to invite chaos. Even today there are major ecclesiastical institutions and not a few nation-states that consider dangerous the idea of free elections, the philosophy of democracy, the sharing of power among various groups of the society in question.

Violence is deeply rooted in human experience and history, as deeply rooted as the tendency to organize the lives of others in monarchical and hierarchical arrangements. Violence is present not only in the aggressive behavior of destructive people but also in the tactics of the superficially nonviolent.

Some are never violent in an overt manner because they have no need to be. They concur in oppression passively and reap the benefits of a society built on violence. For this reason, Merton believed that nonviolence was less a question of behavior than of motivation. The nonviolent person identifies easily with others, especially with those whose human rights are denied by law or by actual fact in unjust societies.

Merton is less radical than his mentor, Mahatma Gandhi, who allows violence under no circumstances. Merton moves in the direction of Latin American liberation theology.

> Those who in some way or other concur in the oppression—and perhaps profit by it—are exercising violence even though they may be preaching pacifism.... If the oppressed try to resist by force—which is their right—theology has no business preaching non-violence to them.[35]

Merton does not define what he means by "force." The passage remains ambivalent. Gandhi and King and Merton concur in the belief that pacifism is not passivity. The nonviolent person has an obligation to be active on behalf of justice. This is to be done forcefully. Otherwise pacifism becomes a means by which cowardice or indifference masquerades under another name. Merton seems to allow more than active resistance, however, in his use of the word *force*.

There is a stern discipline involved in nonviolence. It requires lifelong commitment rather than tactics. If it restrains violence on one level of human action, it demands creative alternatives on other levels. It exposes the unsettling response of trusting the future and the truth even when we do not control them.

Nonviolence seeks an asceticism in which forces and values larger than ourselves are believed to be operative and effective in the structuring of human history. Violence equates truth with a reality entirely of our own making. Such an attitude engenders ceaseless activity; it also encourages violence. In his *Clement of Alexandria*, Merton states the problem succinctly:

> Such a man no longer really believes in the power of truth.... He on the contrary defends the truth as something smaller than himself.[36]

The nonviolent person is expected to be so radical a thinker that conversion of the "wicked" to the ideas of the "good" is not intended. The energy expended to effect such a conversion is frequently the energy of violence and oppression. The nonviolent person seeks instead the indictment of the "wicked" in each of us and the manifestation to the "wicked" of the goodness in them. The imposition of the "best" as a norm for all is tyranny by another name. From Gandhi, Merton learns that the defeat of one's enemy is accomplished not by assault or degradation but by allowing the enemy to become other than the enemy. An adversary is overcome by examining the roots of hostility in the self as well as in the other. There is no question of victory or defeat, merely a question of life in which both parties win and lose.

The nonviolent resister "is fighting for *every*body." The nonviolent do not assume, as the violent often do, that the adversary is impervious to reason or good intentions. Nor do the nonviolent turn the people they oppose to homicidal desperation. Violence is the result not only of the failure of the violent but also of the blindness of the allegedly nonviolent. Ironically, the realist in the situation is the genuinely nonviolent person who does not push people beyond their endurance. The nonviolent are expected to be as aware of the limits of the oppressor as they are conscious of their own goals.

Nonviolence seeks dialogue, not victory. The violent, however, presuppose that the enemy is not worth talking to because the enemy cannot understand in human terms. Merton is not concerned about marginal cases of evil where people become incapable of controlling their destructive obsessions and therefore of talking to others. Merton is concerned with the overwhelming majority of cases that human beings and nation-states face every day.

Merton tried to hold in tension the restraint of nonviolence and its potential for violence. True nonviolence requires spiritual discipline and a deep love for people. It is free from the compulsion to be right or to win. It believes that sooner or later the adversary will see the point and freely move toward nonviolence. Nonviolence seeks the humanity of the oppressor and honors it. It does not intend even the embarrassment of the oppressor.

If pacifism harbors a subtle violence, it leaves in its wake bitterness and anger. It brings nothing new into human affairs but becomes merely the old belligerence with sophisticated and undetectable weapons.

Merton's capacity to see many sides of the same question, his penchant for paradox, enabled him to keep alive a saving dialectic in the construction of a viable nonviolence. His pacifism was not absolute even though his distrust of violence was constant. In his attitude toward nonviolence, he was suspicious of facility and fakery.

Merton's formula for nonviolence is carefully developed. We might conclude this section by summarizing four basic points in his approach. Two of these points concern the attitude of the nonviolent; two of them, the tactics of nonviolence.

Nonviolence is a method to be employed only by those whose strength of character is reliable. The nonviolent must keep in check enormous forces and pressures. Nonviolence must be active without being agitated, pliable without being docile, successful without being acquisitive. Perhaps nonviolence asks too much of us in the present state of our development. It can be nourished, however, by contemplation and compassion, by fasting and love.

The disciple of nonviolence must be as concerned about the adversary as about the self and one's own objectives. Nonviolence seeks to humanize rather than to win, to balance the human equation rather than keep it unsettled. It seeks to renew and reform a situation radically, not by having oppressor and oppressed merely change places, but by eliminating oppression altogether. In its finest expression, nonviolence allows no victory. Perhaps, better, all win.

Nonviolent resistance should not be generic or unfocused. Random action is a characteristic of violent behavior. Resistance should be directed against a particular law, problem, or attitude. The limited character of the resistance should be spelled out, the reasons of noncompliance made clear. The resistance should declare a willingness to accept punishment where its actions are illegal and when its program provokes anger or fear in the hearts of others. The acceptance of the punishment continues the witness. It allows oppressors and observers to see the character of the oppressive behavior. Oppression against the innocent and the vulnerable is eventually self-defeating.

Nonviolence must be mature, well prepared, and disciplined. Its action should never be immoral, self-serving, or consonant with the degradation of the opponent. Nonviolence is planned, not spontaneous; it enlists people, not by their arbitrary choice to join the nonviolent movement but by selection based on their character. Nonviolence is monastic and worldly, spiritual and political, mystical and efficient, poetic and pragmatic. It is a dialectic of secular objectives and religious motives, a venture congenial to East and West, humanist and believer. It is, therefore, deeply unitive and creative. Nonviolence requires that we recognize the nature of evil and choose not to be paralyzed by fear, that we see the potential for goodness in the oppressor and decide not to be immobilized by despair.

Turning East

It is not a large step from trust in nonviolence to sensitivity to Asian religions. The East may have developed more richly than the West a capacity for tolerance, a nonjudgmental approach to life, a spirituality less militant and therefore perhaps more open to the witness of nonviolence. Merton's roots in nonviolence and in the East go back to his early years. Both were abiding interests of his, parallel concerns, always relationally necessary for each other's progress. In the East and its "feminine" approach to life, in the intuitive and gentle dimensions of Asian spirituality, he found the maternal influence he missed. The women in his life, from mother to lover, were never as real to him as the maternity of the East. He was fascinated and frightened by women when they became flesh and blood rather than symbols. The East was his Beatrice. In it he found a light that burned brightly, a light not necessarily better than that of the West but different enough to allow new things to be seen.

Merton's great poems, *Cables to the Ace* and *The Geography of Lograire*, could not have happened without the pilgrimage to the East. Few meetings in his life excited him more than the meeting with D.T. Suzuki, the Zen scholar. The meeting was a perfect paradox. The first long trip outside the monastery, the first return to New York, was made in circumstances he would have thought impossible when he entered the abbey. He traveled east from Kentucky for a meeting that culminated long years of thinking and writing about the East.

Few books meant more to him than his translations of Chuang-tzu and his reflection on the relationship of Zen to Christianity. He repudiated *The Seven Storey Mountain* and called his early poetry inferior, but he voiced no criticisms of his work on the East.

No journey had more meaning for him than his journey to Asia. When he was celebrated there as having already a Buddha nature, he was far more grateful and humbled than he would have been by any Western accolade. He now begins to dream not only the dreams of his earlier years but the dream that he is a Buddhist.

The East answered his psychic and spiritual needs in a way Western Christianity could not fully. It is probable that Cistercian monastic life saved Merton from a life of pessimism. The Catholic tradition does have a unique capacity to engender optimism in the face of evil. Merton required this to balance the somber views of human nature evident in his early novel and subsequent autobiography. As his spiritual life developed, however, he sought relief from the dogmatism and abstraction of Western thought. He wanted a life that was less defined than the West allowed. He turned to the hermitage and to the East, to experience the reality of contemplation rather than its form.

It was especially in Zen that the encounter with reality seemed to go beyond the contradictions of his life. The point, however is not the resolution of the contradictions but the experience of living them so fully that one gets beyond them. Zen pushes the contradictions to their ultimate limit where one has to experience madness or unity. The irony lies in the fact that the contradictions are the essence of the unity and yet seem to resist it.

The relationship between contradiction and consciousness intrigued Merton. Western culture attempts to resolve in the self the contradictions at the heart of reality. It searches for a formula the self can manage so that the self can comprehend the solution of the problem. But reality, as the East envisions it, does not yield to comprehension or to the self. Reality is not grasped by reason but encountered in contemplation and compassion.

The spiritual task presented to human nature involves getting beyond the empirical, the shallow self that requires egocentricity and indulgence for its survival. At a deeper level, there is a real self, a self that harmonizes with other people, with reality, with whatever is absolute. The empirical self isolates us from others and becomes the basis for the roles we play in life. Its fundamental hunger is survival and aggrandizement. The real self seeks a wider world of meaning and yields to it. On the empirical level, life is a question of contradictions and compulsions. On the real level, life is an experience of harmony and peace.

Merton feared that the West had gone too far in adopting a Cartesian approach to life. The West tended to dualism and to the separation of good from evil, truth from error, the self from others, God from creation, one religion from the rest. It concerned itself with decisive victories and precise doctrines. Nonviolence was more congenial to an Eastern outlook on life because it sought a unity beyond triumph or defeat. It sought the real self of the contesting parties, attempting to get beyond the empirical level where conflict occurs.

The emergence of the real self requires suffering and sacrifice. It necessitates a journey to the heart of the self, to the core of the real, a journey which is a crucifixion marked by contradiction before it is made whole by the very contradiction that diminished it. We need universal compassion because all of us are obliged to take this journey to the real self, bear this pain, do this dying. We are fascinated by the thought of pilgrimage because we all belong to the unknown, fated for a silence so deep that it frightens us even as it restores us. The mistake of the West lies in its attempt to find meaning in thinking and in the self; the gift of the East is its insistence that meaning does not result from thinking but from experience and that meaning is never for the self as an individual but for everyone.

> The taste for Zen in the West is in part a healthy reaction of people exasperated with the...flight from being into verbalism, mathematics, and rationalization. Descartes made a fetish out of the mirror in which the self finds itself. Zen shatters it.[37]

Merton's long search for the self terminated paradoxically in the East where the no-self or the nonself is the answer. The reason why nonviolence is difficult for the West is because nonviolence undermines the empirical self on which so much of Western culture is premised. Merton's Eastern pilgrimage is a marriage of Hinduism and Buddhism. From Hinduism he learns about nonviolence; from Buddhism he appreciates why nonviolence is necessary. The loss of the self is the beginning of wisdom and the essence of pacifism.

The Buddhist ability to make us compassionate rests upon its negation of distance and duality. Buddhism does not contain in itself a doctrinal problem that would impede a rapprochement with Christianity. For Buddhism is not "a doctrine but a way of being in the world…not a set of beliefs but an opening to love," Merton wrote in *Zen and the Birds of Appetite.* An abiding sense of the unity possible when people are not violent or selfish was at the heart of Merton's social concerns.

Paradoxically, Buddhism, which has less interest in social justice than does Christianity, brought Merton a renewed sense of social commitment. Evil in society did not derive from experiences like Hiroshima or Auschwitz or Vietnam. These were symptom of a deeper need to be violent and of a compulsion to prefer the self. There will be further symptoms until the underlying problems are addressed. No investigation or reflection on why these atrocities occur will prevent their recurrence unless the more profound aspects of the problems are confronted. Buddhism avoids the Western fascination with transforming persons and social institutions from the outside. It seeks to destroy the barriers of illusion that set up race or nation or even institutional religion as absolutes.

CHAPTER FOUR

A Child Shall Lead Us

Merton maintained his balance in life by searching. His life was a quest for the perfect poem and the perfect prayer. He was young in verse and in contemplation, recovering in both the childhood that prose and history denied him. His lost childhood was the object of his yearning, a childhood richly revealed in *The Seven Storey Mountain*, symbolically relived in *The Geography of Lograire.* His long pilgrimage for a home to settle him was also a journey back to the home he never had as a child.

For Merton, poetry had something to do with the refreshment of the human heart. As his poetry developed, it became religious not in its content but in its capacity to deal with the spirit and encounter the common core of our humanity. As we see in *Bread in the Wilderness,* poetry was for him a reality that "could not be produced by any other combination of words," a work of art that lived a life all its own. The point of the poem was not only aesthetic enchantment but contemplation and dialogue. Poetic experience, like religious experience, is an act of communion with the world. A poem is religious not because its intent is religious but because it intends contact with human meaning on the deepest level possible.

Merton published poetry before he published prose. His poetry precedes his entrance into the Abbey of Gethsemani and helps to establish him there. The poetry and the contemplation converge. The contemplative silence of Merton was not negated by his poetic work. It could be violated only by words that sought no communion. Poetry as monologue would be as empty as contemplative silence limited to self development. The key to literature and the spiritual life is bonding, achieved not by the proclamation of one's ego but by the yielding of the self to the larger meanings of human communion and universal love. Silence is not taciturnity; silence is the time it takes for words to create community.

> It is not speaking that breaks our silence, but the anxiety to be heard. The words of the proud man impose silence on all others, so that he alone may be heard.[38]

Childhood is the experience of life in utter simplicity. Poetry and sanctity are the recovery of that simplicity, achieved not by naiveté and inexperience but by choice. The difference between the simplicity of the child and that of the adult is the difference between inevitability and freedom. The child has no alternative but to remain uncomplex; the adult eliminates complexity by choice.

Poetry, childhood, and sanctity are rooted in the ordinary course of life. The utterly simple poem or parable, the uncomplicated vision of the child, the serenity of the saint are the essence of life. We are charmed by such experiences because life is engaging whenever it avoids artificiality.

The Bible is a good starting point for the recovery of the ordinary. The Bible presents creation in simple terms and, therefore, accounts for the world in poetic language. It invites us to encounter God through life as we already experience it rather than in exotic forms, to find God in problems we have previously addressed rather than in those that exceed our capacity to handle them. This is a constant theme in Merton's theology. The spiritual life originates and develops in life as we already deal with it.

The Bible is a worldly book since the God it encounters is always at the center of familiar human experiences: work and play, family and friends, leisure and love. In our time, "we have lost sight of the fact that even the most ordinary actions of our everyday life are invested, by their nature, with a deep spiritual meaning," he writes in *The Living Bread.* The frequent Merton diatribes against technology are rooted in the fear that the machine may complicate the process by which poetry and prayer are nurtured. It is not the comfort technology brings that is a danger, but the complexity it entails; not the leisure it allows, but the sense it engenders that leisure is not significant. Technology leads us to equate complexity and intelligence. It encourages us to suppose that life is better managed by experts than by poets or saints. It seduces academic life, even theology, into assuming that gravity and complication are the essence of wisdom. The spiritual renewal of our era originates in the need to make our lives human once again.

"For me," Merton writes in *Seeds of Contemplation,* "to be a saint means to be myself." To be holy is a question of appreciating where one is in life and learning to foster the vital connections that are already operative. Sanctity is an experience of freedom nurtured in a sense of humor that finds pretense and pomposity ridiculous. A saint deals with life lightly. "I snap the fingers at life," Merton writes to his good friend Bob Lax. Gravity is a spiritual malady, a symptom of the death of the heart. The recovery of simplicity was for Merton a question of desire. We always become the things we truly wish to be. Heaven begins and ends with the hopes of the human heart. This "inner paradise" becomes the "ultimate ground of freedom.... To find it one had to travel, as Augustine had said, not with steps but with yearnings." The journey is less demanding than we imagine. Nothing that we choose, he observes laconically in *Cables to the Ace,* is beyond our capacity to bear it.

For this reason, Merton believed that effort and difficulty were the adversaries of spiritual development. We can become so intent on good and proper responses that the point of our spiritual search becomes not God but our own devotion. There was always something natural and unforced about the asceticism of Merton. He could be difficult to live with and cantankerous at times. His occasional irascibility was due, not to his asceticism or sacrifice, but to the unique blend of his personal idiosyncrasies and his artistic temperament.

Our knowledge of God derives from an experience of our dependence rather than from learning new things about God. God intensifies the dependence by revealing divinity to us in ways that cancel each other out. The God we seek "rises up out of the sea like a treasure in the waves," he writes in *Thoughts in Solitude*. When language and intelligence falter before the vision, "His brightness remains on the shores of our own being" in silence. God is an encounter with a love so expansive that we are frightened by it. We sense fear because we know we depend upon and belong to a love that exceeds, impoverishes, and encircles our resources all at once. Love is "the epiphany of God in our poverty."

When Merton's words sing with poetic resonance, his contemplative vocation develops. Merton was convinced that we suffer reverses in the spiritual life not because our desires are uncontrolled but because our humanity is deficient.

> That is why the stern asceticism that was devised to control violent passions may do more harm than good when it is applied to a person whose emotions have never properly matured and whose instinctual life is suffering from weakness and disorder.[39]

Merton's answer to a disappointing experience in prayer is more expansive human experience rather than greater effort or new techniques. In this, Merton shows himself the son of Bernard of Clairvaux the contemplative as well as the son of Owen Merton the artist. Prayer has a closer affinity to passion than to procedure.

The spiritual life is built from the simple materials that make poetry and life joyful. It has something to do with acceptance of self and of the situation in which we find ourselves. When we doubt our existence at a fundamental level, we turn frantically to activity, to achievement in place of acceptance. We use action to justify our existence when we no longer believe in it. Activity is part of the Western tendency to externalize the entire reality of life, to make meaning dependent on realities less important than human life. This makes us, in effect, two people. It is the less fortunate result of Western dualism. Schizophrenia keeps us in conflict with ourselves, in competition with ourselves, unknown to ourselves. We remain unaware of the deeper or real self in us whose function it is to humanize and unify.

This tendency creates in us an expectation for serenity from things alien to human development. Material affluence is equated not only with the worth of our possessions but with our worth as persons. Affluence, however, has built into it a frantic, frustrating, self-contradictory potential. It excites useless activity in search of purposeless wealth, withdrawing us from life, generating in us a subconscious death wish. One seeks to surpass one's neighbor, rejoices in the diminishment of one's associates, delights in the losses others sustain even though this brings no advantage. We do these things because we are restless with ourselves, bored with life, threatened by others, addicted to externals.

A life derived from a need to succeed with one's actions rather than with the self makes the other person a competitor. We hunger for success, which easily becomes a way of intruding on the lives of others.

Merton was fond of relating a story Chuang-tzu told many centuries ago. It concerned one's reaction to a boat that might collide with one's own. If there is someone in the other boat we become angry. We react this way because another ego has gotten in our way. We hold people responsible for limiting our freedom to act as long as there is someone near us to blame. If, however, there is no one in the boat that has struck us we are not likely to become angry.

The point of the story concerns the need to empty ourselves of our obtrusive ego. If people find in us a person full of self, they are threatened by our success or by our obstruction. But if we empty our boat, so to speak, of ourselves, we cross the rivers of life with little opposition or harm. In this sense, success is the beginning of failure; fame is the first step toward disgrace.

Eventually, the hunger for success leads us to reduce the energy and rhythm of our lives to planning. We do not live; we calculate. Life becomes an obsession in which we try to get something for ourselves out of everything. This makes it psychologically impossible for us to give without counting the cost or estimating some benefit from the giving. The more we have, ironically, the less we may give.

When we organize life too tightly, we destroy it. System has a way of making us excessively self-conscious. Chuang-tzu reminds us that when a shoe fits, the foot is forgotten. When life is lived properly, the effort and the activity are not arduous. The Church may reinforce the obsessions of the secular world when it forces us into systems, when it neglects the need of our nature for different drummers, more congenial spiritualties, a new set of viable options. Regimentation is a sign that life has gone and we are left with lifestyle.

Merton required simplicity in his personal life and elevated this experience to a principle in his spiritual theology. His own life had once been a frenetic effort to force meaning into a deteriorating sense of self. Sex and alcohol had become substitutes for living. There was something desperate about him in those early days. The word most often used to describe him was "wild." The wildness masked a fear that his life had no future, that his hopes for friendship and love would never be realized. Even in the monastery the old obsessions returned. The need to write reached near-neurotic proportions and Merton turned at times from the compulsion to write, in anger and disgust.

There were other drives. Although young in his monastic vocation, he sought to change its form radically by living the life of a hermit. The hermitage became in his mind an escape from his need to remain excessively active. When he began to get permission to travel outside the monastery, he wanted to go everywhere. He would have traveled to excess had he the opportunity. He was a man, despite his disclaimers to the contrary, who needed strong personalities to settle him.

There were, furthermore, the journals. Merton wrote a great deal about himself and his life. It is surprising that he kept such detailed journals. More astonishing is the fact that he wished them to be published in all their candor and searching honesty. He was driven to produce and especially to publish. The pressure was his way of convincing himself that he was truly alive, that his course was right, his heart pure, his vocation intact.

Merton argued that there is a need for asceticism in the human spirit. He felt the need in his own life. If we do not deny ourselves in creative ways, we punish ourselves in a destructive manner. American culture, especially, drives us to a compulsive need to work and a desperate need to continually improve our lives. We are driven to overcome past deficiencies with future successes, to recoup all the losses of life, to win for the sheer exhilaration of winning, to crowd into each lifetime every experience possible, even those that are patently contradictory and inevitably counterproductive.

Deep within Merton was a guilt he never did fully exorcise. It had something to do with his brother and his parents, with the women he had loved, with the people he regarded too lightly along the way. The guilt fueled a spectacular conversion, as *The Seven Storey Mountain* amply demonstrates. The guilt served another creative role in his life. It gave Merton a sensitivity to his contemporaries and to their problems in accepting themselves. The guilt was slowly transformed into contemplation and compassion. But it seldom allowed him to feel good about himself. And so the need to punish himself with an asceticism turned into excessive activity was always there.

The vividness and perception that mark Merton's spiritual writing derive from the keenness with which he felt the issues in his own person. The ease he sought was not the same as comfort. He had proved, both in sin and sanctity, that he could absorb enormous punishment. In his secular years, so to speak, he was capable of excesses that moved beyond pleasure into genuine pain. In his monastic years he was able to handle amounts of work that would have felled most people with exhaustion and illness. He came perilously close to complete nervous fatigue a number of times. His physical system rebelled against the tyrannical commitments to which he subjected his life. He was continually ill, often with maladies born of stress and tension.

Simplicity beckoned to him as a redeemer. He reduced his possessions and circumscribed his autonomy; he confined himself physically to Gethsemani. It helped for a time, but the complications returned. He sometimes gave the impression that he did not know himself, and he blamed others for the lack in himself.

His works are filled with criticisms of a life of frenzy and sharp descriptions of how affluence kills, possessions suffocate, power erodes. Toward the end of his life he gained access to the hermitage and, for awhile, the silence heals and the furies are set at rest. But it begins again as he plunges into his wild but brilliant poem, *The Geography of Lograire.* He becomes restless for the journey to Asia. He crowds into the journey enough travel and talks, experience and interviews, journal writing and correspondence to strain his physical and emotional health. He becomes ill on the trip and begins to wonder if the trip is worthwhile. He asks himself if there was anything new to discover that he had not already known.

But God must come to us in simple ways, he reasons. God is not in the whirlwind or in the flame. God is the still point behind the wind and the fire. Merton had trouble reaching that center. Every cell of his body strained for peace and yearned to be settled.

He wanted to be a child again, to begin the journey once more, to start out with people and God and do it better. His poetry was his way of returning. The early poetry is charming in its naïveté and gracious simplicity. He is enthralled by sunlight and glass, by snow and wheat, by the grass of the fields and the grace of faith, by wine and worship. The later poetry becomes more complicated. There is a harshness in *Emblems of a Season of Fury* that was absent in *Thirty Poems.* There is a confusion in *Cables to the Ace* and *The Geography of Lograire* that differs markedly from the clarity of *A Man in the Divided Sea.*

The genius of Merton lay in his capacity to renew his simplicity despite encroaching complexity. In this lay also the secret of his mysticism. The yearning for Asia was a longing to get beyond the duality of Western thought. The hermitage was a way of becoming a child again. His contemplative vocation helped him to come out fresh again despite the staleness of his neurotically encumbered life. For this reason, he clings to prayer and to his vocation. He speaks hardly a word about the priesthood in all his writings; the priesthood is a more complicated form of life than monasticism. Monasticism reduces life to more fundamental categories of home and stability, relationship and community life, equal sharing and manual labor. Merton is an appealing mystic because we sense in his spiritual journey all the complications of our era and yet come away convinced that simplicity and spirituality are accessible.

Merton's emotional tension made him unusually perceptive about dangers and obstacles in the spiritual life. Early in his writing, he warns about the avidity, almost the greed, some people have for exterior and dramatic renunciation. The apparent punishment becomes a reverse pleasure. Such asceticism leads nowhere because it is self-conscious, insensitive to contact with deeper realities in the self where we become conscious of universal connections. It is isolated from God and human life, lost in a cycle that spirals into actions where punishment and pleasure constantly succeed each other but never lead to a further step in the journey toward a fuller life.

The desire for punishment is sometimes transformed into a need to punish others. In parenting or political life, in academic or ecclesiastical circles, there emerges a personality that identifies truth with discomfort, grace with suffering, loyalty with submission. Such personalities are threatened by people who live life with relative ease and a degree of freedom, with success won, not from effort, but from a serenity and creativity that transcend all systems.

There are religious people, Merton observes, who pray best when they imagine themselves rejected by a fierce and implacable God. Their spiritual life consists in their acceptance of this rejection as a value in its own right. They become uncomfortable whenever they feel good about themselves. Correlatively, there are people in the Church who foster this attitude. They require perfection from others and accuse them of failure when it does not come to pass. The search for human development, the desire for options, the satisfactions that come from sources not sanctioned by the official Church are judged indulgent. Many Catholics become insecure about their encounter with Christ if it takes a form not yet officially approved. They become uncertain about the decisions they make in their own conscience if such a conscience does not have magisterial support.

For Merton, the spiritual life is free of constraint. His description of the liberty love brings is poetic, a sign that something deep within him corresponded to the notion of freedom. The freedom he seeks is obviously the freedom of the spirit.

> Here there is no darkness. The dawn has come.... The soul stands on the bank of another Jordan—the bright calm river of death. It looks across the river and sees the clear light upon the mountains of the true promised land. It begins to be ravished to the depths of its being by the clean scent of forests full of spice and balsam. It stands upon the river bank with the wonderful soft wind of the New World playing upon its cheeks and upon its eyelids and in its hair.[40]

Youth and poetry, childhood and prayer, simplicity and spiritual yearning combine in this passage. It is Merton at his best. The book just quoted, *The Ascent to Truth,* is not an especially good one, although Merton worked on it more ardently than perhaps on any other. This may be why the book does not succeed. There is little spontaneity or vitality in it. The book fails because it is forced into a Scholastic frame of reference. When the book breaks free of Scholastic categories, as it does in the above passage, it is momentarily quite effective.

For Merton, prayer is a natural, not a contrived, process. The dialectic in his thought is evident as he probes the mystery of prayer and seeks ways for it to release creative energy in his own life and in the lives of others. We have seen that Merton insists that prayer be improved not by technique but by expanding and enriching human experience. The naturalness in prayer is evident in Merton's answer to the problem of distractions. People who have no distractions, he wisely observes, do not know how to pray. Prayer must move with the rhythm of life. Life is a circular and tentative process. Paradoxically, the single-minded person has not simplified life but complicated it. Prayer naturally drifts into distraction. The prayer continues as we quietly come back to the point.

Genuine prayer addresses a balance in the human psyche, not a distorted equation that makes the ambivalence of human life impossible by reducing all its elements to one factor. And so distractions are part of prayer. The simplicity of the human heart demands that prayer follow an uncomplicated course if both the heart and prayer are to be nourished. Rigid structures suffocate prayer. They sometimes do this perfecting the technique of prayer and leaving the experience of prayer underdeveloped.

This is not to suggest, however, that prayer is nothing more than instinct. Despite appearances to the contrary, prayer seeks structure and system. These get in the way of prayer only when people forget that the most striking characteristic of human life is the personal dimension. The personal is always unique. In nature, we are the same; as persons, we are distinct. The structure each seeks must be a structure that takes into account our difference from all the others who pray.

Merton makes these observations during his Asian journey. It is fitting. The East has gifted the world with the experience of Tao, the Way, by which all opposites are given their place. Structure and spirit, spontaneity and system must be given their due. The dynamics by which life moves forward in Taoism is not by means of progress but by a stable and serene immobility. One goes forward by remaining still and yet is quiet by constant activity.

In any case, the contemplative is not the person who takes prayer seriously but the person who is serious about God. A contemplative is anxious for the truth, not for the means by which it is achieved or the recognition received in its attainment. The spiritual life is an uncharted region. No matter how much knowledge or support one has as the journey is begun, each must walk into the unknown. Neither life nor God, not even the self, are quantifiable. In this realm, losses become part of the gain because God seeks a total person rather than an ideal order. It is not perfection that matters but trying to give oneself totally, with all the defects and the successes. The human heart sometimes fails to resonate with life or with the grace of God because it is cluttered with the clichés of spiritual books or the imperatives of spiritual systems.

Method and Prayer

Elaborate methods of prayer began to flourish in the fifteenth and sixteenth centuries, Merton observes. At this time, enthusiasm for the development of the scientific method was intense. Prayer also became an object of observation. It was subjected to laboratory experiments in which different methods were used in an attempt to discover which of them was best. The scientific need for general laws explaining all specific instances of a certain order was transformed into a spiritual need for universal principles capable of sanctifying everyone in the same way. Prayer, however, is closer to poetry than to science. Poetry is inspired not by general laws but by specific instances, concerned not with universal principles but with individual realities. Science seeks the universal rather than the particular, the species rather than the person, the norm rather than the exception, the timeless truth rather than its perishable expression. Prayer is meant to be, like poetry, concrete in its concern. It is akin to childhood, which is specific in all its perceptions. It is consonant with simplicity, which is singular and irreducible.

The laboratory setting was too artificial for the kind of prayer Merton encouraged. Prayer works better, Merton would insist, in a hermitage. The act of merely waking up in a hermitage is itself a prayer. The heart, sensing gratitude and joy, achieves contemplation in simplicity and without arduous effort. The most ordinary actions we perform are the most sublime. They are natural to us. This is why we do not tire of them, why we repeat them endlessly in life. A contrived action, however, wears us out; exotic or elaborate realities quickly become tedious.

Merton was moved to poetry by ordinary tasks in the hermitage because his prayer was uncomplicated. He writes of rain in beautiful images. Rain is a festival. The child in us comes alive in a rainfall. It leads us to celebrate the gratuitousness and grace, the freedom and privilege of the surrounding rain. Rain engulfs us and passes beyond our control.

Merton begins to relax in the hermitage the way he had not unwound in his entire life. In the wilderness, as he calls it, he learns to sleep again because he no longer feels alien. The hermitage represents home. He is reconciled to himself. This makes him want to touch the deer as they approach his home. Merton speaks little of touching in his earlier writing. The prose and poetry are remarkably devoid of embraces or kisses. The child in him always needed physical contact. His mother, dying, left him without an embrace; the warmth of his father was expressed in paints and colors and words but not in touches. Something in Merton was never healed because of his fear of human contact. As Merton unwinds, a new creative energy unites him with the universe and makes him want to touch it and be touched by it. "The trees I know, the night I know, the rain I know."

Merton's human experience is enriched in the hermitage and his prayer life become more telling. It becomes engagingly simple. "Where rain, sunlight and darkness are contemned, I cannot sleep," he writes in *Raids on the Unspeakable.* He is far now from the incessant machinery of the monastery, from the regimen of Cistercian life. The Trappist lifestyle once helped, but now a certain distance from it seems necessary. Softness and tenderness enter his heart. The rain, the deer, the fragrance of darkness, the music of daylight settle him. It is a good place to be—a good place for a poet, for a mystic. He falls in love while living as a hermit. But this disturbs nothing because he has learned to be vulnerable in new and creative ways.

"Thoreau sat in *his* cabin and criticized the railways. I sit in mine and wonder about a world that has, well, progressed," Merton continues in *Raids.* He is alone in the metaphorical desert of the heart, in the wilderness of the human spirit. All the fears of death and the needs for self-affirmation are seen as illusions and vanish from his concern. Merton is a child again in the hermitage and the adult fears slip away; he is a contemplative and the anxieties diminish. Merton encounters peace "in the heart of anguish." He takes on the "universal anguish" of the human race and becomes through it an apostle commissioned by his pain to proclaim universal love.

In this simplicity, won from the years of labor and hope, he finds new meaning in nonviolence. It is possible, he observes, to live without the need to kill and even without the need for a doctrine that permits killing with a good conscience. He quotes Philoxenos, a sixth-century Syrian hermit: "It is not he who has many possessions that is rich, but he who has no needs." He learns to need only the moment he has.

Merton has made a ritual from the simple realities of life, festival from the rhythms of nature, prayer from waking and walking, from looking and touching, from sleeping and dreaming. There is a convergence in the hermitage of all the influences in his life that promised simplicity if they were properly nurtured: the poverty into which he was born; the soft colors with which his father painted landscapes and sunlight; the love for Francis of Assisi and the desire to become a Franciscan; the train ride to Gethsemani as he left behind all he had accomplished; the life of Cistercian simplicity and the spare sublimity of Zen Buddhism; the home he finds at last in the hermitage; the uncomplicated character of his best prose and poetry; the unpretentiousness of his better journals.

The tasks he performs to keep the hermitage in order become a spiritual experience in their own right. In a style reminiscent of Ernest Hemingway, he speaks of washing the dishes carefully, of cleaning the pot, each knife and spoon, of letting water renew the cup and bowl. He does not rush his sensations, as Hemingway would say. He gives each element in his life its due. He respects the order he finds; by caring for it, he is drawn mysteriously into its larger meaning. In Merton, the improbable convergence of Zen Buddhism and Ernest Hemingway occurs. It is quintessential Merton to harmonize the unthinkable. The point of contact in this case is not only the man who loves both Zen and Hemingway but the careful attention Zen and Hemingway give to the most ordinary tasks in the process of living.

Reflections on Materialism

The simplicity Merton achieves makes him perceptive about problems that impede spiritual and human development. Hypocrisy, he observes, is a danger in contemporary life because affluence has taken away our sense of gratitude. Gratitude creates sincerity because it evades pretense; it reinforces frugality because one is satisfied with all that life has already given. It leads, therefore, to poverty.

Greed takes many forms when gratitude is lacking. There is greed in the idolatry of work and in the passion for achievement in modern secular life, Merton observes. There is, furthermore, a reverse materialism in the religious life, which makes people suspect that abnegation requires the surrender of things that gratify the senses. This leads some to deny their humanity in order to exercise a greed in terms of the spirit.

Actually, holiness and humanness both require a delight in the senses. When life loses its simplicity, spirituality can become so complicated that the obvious need for the senses in human development is denied. When gratitude is deficient, we seek to make ourselves something different from all other people by fostering an elitism of the spirit. Beneath the surface, we are seeking power and attention by means of a bizarre spiritual program. The New Testament moves in another direction. It describes Jesus as someone who delights in wine, who speaks tenderly of wheat and rain, who invites the disciples to leisure on the lakeshore, and to a Passover celebration in the Upper Room.

"Nothing is more suspicious in a man who seems holy, than an impatient desire to reform other men."[41] We do not need liberation from the body in Western civilization. Indeed, we have not learned to be grateful for our bodies. We torture them with repression of sensual pleasure in one era and an excess of sensual pleasure in the next. In ecclesiastical life, some trade sensual pleasure for spiritual power, surrender affluence but not aggrandizement, destroy the lives of others, not by competition but by control. Spiritual excellence is best revealed in the person who surrenders power and allows others to exist in their own right.

Merton began to write critically and caustically against materialism and technology around the time of his conversion. His voice is sometimes shrill. Merton's concern is not with the indulgence involved in affluence. There is little trace of his anger at those who seek pleasure. The problem is rooted, he believes, in the blockage materialism creates for the deeper creative dimensions of human life.

The influence of his recent conversion and the seeds of his growing mysticism can be detected in the thesis Merton writes for his master's degree at Columbia in English literature. The subject is William Blake, but the scope of the work includes reflections on mysticism and the artistic process. The year is 1939; he is young, but already Merton sees that materialism wastes human life. Consumption and contemplation are not harmonious.

The thesis is about Blake, but it is especially about those elements in Blake's life and work that are most like Merton's. He speaks of the Augustinianism of Blake, of the protest of the poet against his century, a protest deriving from his mysticism.

Contemplation took Merton beyond protest into communion. Genuine contemplation is always a social experience, no matter how solitary it seems to be. It is a quest not for the self but for the reality beyond the self. It leads the contemplative to compassionate connection with the lives of others. In loneliness, almost beyond bearing, there is life totally beyond comprehension. After years of searching and suffering, one sees in a moment the whole and knows how easy it might have been to have seen this earlier.

We are diminished in many conventional approaches to the spiritual life because we neglect the process by which each of us is meant to become a mystery of solitude and communion. A metaphor for this reality is the simple experience of a family meal. The meal is a process of solitude since nourishment is an individual endeavor. But the solitude is also a mystery of communion, a celebration of love and union. It is not the body that is nourished at a meal but the whole person. There is more. It is not the whole person alone that is fed but the community that gathers.

The sacrifice demanded of us for a religious life is the same sacrifice required for a human life. Life is not human when life is withheld. The measure of creative sacrifice is never the amount of pain sustained but the power the sacrifice generates to break down walls of isolation and division. The meaning of life is apparent, not in a clear formula but in its lived simplicity. Likewise, the meaning of a poem is not in the information it provides. A poem is rich in its associations and in the resonance it effects. It puts things together, even contradictory things, not so that they can be grasped but so that we might see that they belong. A good poem, like an effective prayer, invites one to give attention and affectivity to life that might otherwise have been neglected.

The waste of life—this is what poetry impedes and prayer prevents. The simplicity born from poetry and prayer is the act of resistance we make to the loss of life. In simplicity, we let things be. We take nothing away. In the gathering, all the contradictions converge: life and death, joy and pain, light and darkness, the world and the Church, East and West, man and woman, adult and child. Nothing is clear because everything is present. The simplicity is the experience that there are no differences for a reason impossible to comprehend.

Merton's search for spiritual grace was a journey back to his childhood and an ardent wish to recapture its innocence and simplicity. He had to work through the heartache of his mother's death, the lack of a stable home, and the tragic end of his father's death, the lost opportunities and permanent guilt of his relationship with his brother. He struggled to distance himself from the searing rejection of the early years at school. He remembered, with an uncanny capacity for recall, every lonely night in the French boarding schools and all the unhappy days in New York as a child.

The return to childhood began with his baptism in New York of all places, the new birth, the vocation to the monastery. He would leave the world and break into it again by a second birth process in Gethsemani. In this new life, he finds the home denied to him in childhood. He strives to make everything simple and he rejoices in the creative renunciation. When the process of purging appears complete, he learns to speak and begins his career in writing. The best writing in his autobiography centers around his years as a child and his early years in the monastery. He links them together and begins a twenty-year cycle of writing that is bewildering in its massiveness. He takes delight in the recognition his work receives because it cancels out the neglect of his childhood. He holds fast to friendships because he had lost so soon and so tragically all three members of his family.

The prayer and the poetry become sacraments of permanent belonging. His childhood is secure as long as they are intact. In the hermitage, they reach a new level of aliveness. As he turns East, the possibility of eternal newness seems assured. He is happy at the end. He dies young, but there is more than tragedy in the dying. He has reached maturity in his heart. Age in the spiritual life is a simple number with no capacity to compound. He grows old in his childhood and young in his dying. He comes home at the end with the pain and the length of the journey behind him.

CHAPTER FIVE

A Cable to Absalom and Abel

The journey from New York State to Kentucky was joyful and sad. It was joyful because a dream was about to be realized. Thomas Merton was going home. It was sad because a life was ending and there was no guarantee that further life would take its place.

Tuesday evening, December 9, 1941. Pearl Harbor was attacked two days earlier. Thomas Merton leaves Olean Station, New York. The trip to Gethsemani begins at night and is marked by freezing rain. Twenty-seven years later he will be buried in the freezing December rain of Gethsemani. Now he is alone. When he is buried, however, the world watches.

It rained when his mother died. He was alone then, too. They left him alone in the car as they went into a large, ugly building. He was six years old. But he remembers well the rain and the tears, the terrible, endless painful tears. He remembers the rain dripping from the roof of the hospital to the roof of the car. He recalls all the sounds and smells and sights of that dreadful day: the sounds of rain and of inconsolable sorrow; the sickening smell of the hospital and the stuffiness of the car; the mist and smoke in the sky and the soot on the black brick building.

This is a chapter about origins that never end, about beginnings that never cease. It will retrace Merton's faint memories of a mother who died when her son was young, but it will deal more tellingly with a son's remembrance of his father. It will speak of the loss between them, a loss like David's of his son Absalom—the fathers in question never knew how to express their affection for their sons. And it will treat of a brother who learned too late that he was meant to be his brother's keeper. John Paul is the Abel in our application of this myth not because Thomas was savage with his brother but because he never learned how to be responsible for him. He lost a brother by inadvertence.

As we shall see, the origins say much about the endings. They say more about the words Thomas used along the way, about the themes he favored and the causes he espoused and the friends he made and the poems he sang. One of these, some say his best, is written in tears at Gethsemani for the fallen flier, the "Icarus" of *The Geography of Lograire.* John Paul is Icarus and Abel. His plane crashes into the North Sea and he is severely injured. His neck is broken; he is in a state of delirium, with a terrible thirst. He begs for water but his companions have none to give him. He suffers three hours of torture and dies. Four days later his friends bury him at sea. Water that gives no life but takes it away.

We have said a word about the "Absalom" and "Abel" in the title of this chapter. The "cable" in the title is the message, the meaning, of the metaphors we use. It is borrowed from Merton's intriguing poem *Cables to the Ace.*

"Sweet brother," he writes in a tender poem when he hears of the death. He never used those words when his brother lived. And now everything in his heart wants his brother to hear them. But it is too late. "Sweet brother." Brothers seldom talk that affectionately to one another. "Sweet brother." Thomas Merton never talked that way except in his dreams or waking reveries, perhaps in a journal, or occasionally in a poem. But not when a person could hear and see the need.

When Thomas Merton writes *The Seven Storey Mountain*, his brother is long dead. But the memories are vivid and unhealed. The first recollections of the lost brother are drawn from the deepest recesses of the author's psyche:

> When I think now...of my childhood, the picture I get of my brother John Paul is this: standing in a field...where we have built our hut, is this little perplexed five-year-old kid in short pants and a kind of leather jacket, standing quite still, with his arms hanging down at his sides, and gazing in our direction, afraid to come any nearer on account of the stones, as insulted as he is saddened, and his eyes full of indignation and sorrow...there he stands, not sobbing, not crying but angry and unhappy and offended and tremendously sad. And yet he is fascinated by what we are doing, nailing shingles all over our new hut. And his tremendous desire to be with us and to do what we are doing will not permit him to go away. The law written in his nature says that he must be with his elder brother, and to do what he is doing: and he cannot understand why this law of love is being so wildly and unjustly violated in his case. Many times it was like that.[42]

The incident related in isolation from the entire context of the fraternal relationship is not singular. Children, in countless cases, repeat the patterns of rejection and absorb the exclusion without damage. Merton sketches the scene vividly because it represents for him a constant failure.

It is a home Thomas is building, a playful one, of course, but one from which he excludes his younger brother. In a later home, the hermitage, near the end of his life, he remembers his brother in tenderness as he writes his journal. In his epic poem, he remembers his brother again.

The poignancy of the passage we have quoted above is intensified by Merton's final recollection of his brother. John Paul, now in uniform, comes to visit his brother at the monastery, and Thomas tries vainly to signal him.

> John Paul was nowhere in sight.
>
> I turned around. At the end of the long nave, with its empty choir stalls.... John Paul was kneeling all alone. He seemed to be an immense distance away... I couldn't call out to tell him how to come down.... And he didn't understand my sign.... At that moment, there flashed into my mind, all the scores of times...I had chased John Paul away.
>
> The next day he was gone.... As the car was turning...John Paul turned around and waved, and it was only then that his expression showed...that we would never see each other on earth again.[43]

As so often with Merton, life comes full circle. The things that matter most are repeated, seldom resolved. With John Paul, the repetitions are more complex. Not only do they evoke the memory of the dead brother, but they provide the opening for his social protest and his secular involvement. Thomas is resolved that he will never again let a brother slip through his life without adequate love. And so he labors on behalf of freedom for victims of poverty and injustice and for those trapped in war. For many, this seems a departure from his former interests; for Thomas, it is consistent with an early love whose expression he frustrated too severely.

Aloneness

Thomas Merton was forced by circumstances to be alone often in his life. After a time, the loneliness became a habit and the problem with affectionate expression insuperable. During the long silences, Merton had grown accustomed to listening to the inner voices of his heart. When Merton turned to mysticism and later to Zen Buddhism, it was in part a desire born of the need to hear other voices in his silence. The Cistercian community and later the hermitage healed some of the shattered pieces of an uprooted life. But the healing came late and needed more time than he was given.

The first loss in his life was that of his mother. Thomas did not remember the relationship as a happy one. Abbot James Fox recalls the "tremendous struggles" of Merton's life and attributes them, in large measure, to the fact of his never having known a mother's love. Although Abbot Fox and Merton were frequently in conflict, the abbot had good reason to know a great deal about Merton. He was Merton's abbot for twenty of his twenty-seven years in the monastery. He went to confession to Thomas Merton for fifteen years.

Ruth Merton kept careful records of her son's childhood. She notes that he is precocious, observant, a very visual person. She is perceptive enough to note in the one-year-old Merton a love of books, a distrust of things manual, an acute sensitivity to nature, and a reluctance to be held. He followed her around the house, imitated things she did very soon after she did them and verbalized about these and other matters with a remarkable facility. We do not wish to deal here with the mother-son relationship in terms explored in a previous chapter. The point of our present inquiry is a search for elements in the origins of Thomas Merton's life that account for his later development as a writer and mystic.

In Merton's autobiography there is a brief scene giving an insight into Merton at a moment of crisis. He returns to New York City to give his spiritual counselor, Fr. Edmund, a full account of his life. He would have been accepted as a Franciscan if he did not choose to be candid. He suspects strongly that his application will be rejected, a suspicion that proves to be correct. He watches a boy who had been swimming run up a path through tall grass, eluding a threatening thunderstorm. The boy's mother calls to him from the porch of the house, and Merton writes of his own terrible sense of homelessness. He is devastated by the inability to pursue his vocation. The pain reminds him of a deeper anguish. His own mother never really called him to her. She informed him in writing rather than by touches and tears that she would soon die and that he was not to be allowed to see her until it was finished. After the letter, he recalls only the scene outside the crematorium, again in the rain, again kept at a distance, again excluded.

There were the many dreams of women. We made reference to them at the beginning of the first chapter. They seem to have been an amalgam of the lost mother and the abiding love he never found. They seem to be allegories of deeper needs, symbols of psychic wounds. At one point the woman is black and he is her son. He feels her embrace him with love, senses gratitude and relief, recognizes in her the warmth of her maternal heart. At the time, he experiences a family bond with oppressed black Americans. He fulfills in them his vow never to let a brother perish by neglect. The dream gathers the loose threads of a mother's love and a son's concern for the other members of the family, of a feminine influence and a trustworthy woman, of a brother who needs assistance and a brother who hears and answers. It is a dream about losses sustained along the way and of Thomas's inability to account for them.

There is a dream of a Jewish girl. He writes to Boris Pasternak about her. He tells the Nobel laureate that he dreamed often of a young teenage girl. Her name was "Proverb." She embraced him often, an embrace of pure affection. He believed he encountered "Proverb" wherever he found beauty, purity, and shyness in people.[44]

An interpretation of Merton's life and writing cannot be limited to a quest for logical connections. His biography is itself poetic, filled with portents and metaphors, laden with nuance and subtlety.

The evasion of logic is explicit. In his late poem *Cables to the Ace*, he observes that the door of hell is inscribed with the word *therefore*. By this he intends a criticism of the logical formula that concludes a syllogism with the code word *therefore* or *ergo*. Logic is the language of hell in the Merton vocabulary. We are seldom more unreasonable than when we demand that everyone be reasonable. In *Cables to the Ace*, he observes: "Cables are never causes."

The key to Merton's thought resides in a close examination of his own life. He had a sense that an answer to the dilemmas of the century lay in himself. There was no arrogance in this, merely a quiet recognition of the fact that he embodied the tensions and sensed the dynamisms of a turbulent era. He understood the language of its pain, the electric shock of its excited joyfulness, the rhythms of its solitude and speech. In *Cables to the Ace*, he says quite simply: "I am the incarnation of everybody…." There is something Whitmanesque and typically American in the line.

Merton had a burning desire to work out his destiny in his own way; in that destiny he read his vocation, his sanctity, his relationship with the world. To live his life more conventionally, even in ecclesiastical terms, represented a betrayal of himself, an infidelity to God, an abandonment of his responsibility to others.

Owen Merton

The beginnings of his life, as we have seen throughout this book, were not promising. In *Cables to the Ace*, he speaks of making the best of rather bad beginnings in the hope that somehow the end will be better. This is quintessential Merton. The observation is eschatological in its intent, referring to all human history, a history marked by a bad beginning in the Fall but a history destined for a redemptive resolution. In the end, it will be better. But the comment is also an apt parallel to the life of Merton, whose beginnings are bad but whose outcome is hopeful. To Robert Lax, his close friend, he writes late in his life that everything will be heard right sometime, by someone.

The problem he faces is the need to say it right with his life. He strives to overcome the loneliness and the incipient despair that become the death of hope. In *Cables to the Ace*, a poem dedicated to Robert Lax, he confesses that he wants no more of his wild hopes to die of affliction. The theme of the entire poem is loneliness. He fears that there may not be enough words to make community happen or that, if there are, he may not be able to find them quickly enough. He labors to decode the opposites in his life, to write down the silences. He is "tormented by poetry and loss." The cable or messages of the poem and of his life seem to make no connections. Nonetheless, he will not despair. "The seed is not afraid of winter...." In an earlier section, he writes:

> What have the signs promised on the lonely hill? Word and work have their measure and so does pain. Look in your own life and see if you find it.[45]

In the bleakness he experiences, Merton reflects on the complete poverty of the Creator from which everything springs. There is at the heart of God an inexhaustible void, an infinite zero, but from this desert of nothing everything takes its origin.

Cables to the Ace is a search for Merton's own origins, for his history and roots. Together with *The Geography of Lograire* and *The Asian Journal*, it forms a trilogy of sorts in a desperate final effort to define the self.

The psychological center of *Cables to the Ace* occurs in Section 20, Parts (a) and (b). In 20a, an appeal is made to the sons in the world that they not become numb. It is a section in which a son is abandoned by a father who is slain. It speaks of being all alone, of a younger brother, of life reduced to "a migrant flame." The flame feeds on nothing; the persona of the poem is not a prophet but an anti-prophet whose life is "a dry homeless tree."

The poem is written during the difficult years we had occasion to speak of earlier. Section 20b is more revealing, perhaps more crucial to the life of Merton and to the meaning of the poem. It is not an appeal to sons that they be not numb but an appeal for the study of history. The section evokes tender images of homecoming and rootedness. It summons Jesus Christ, Huckleberry Finn, James Joyce, Odysseus. It is a brilliant tour de force poetically, a powerful passage psychologically.

It may be beneficial to quote the passage in its entirety:

> Finn, Finn.
> Tribal and double
> Wide awake rocks
> The fatal craft
> Cutlash Finn
> To kill time
> Before and aft—
> er he sinks his fin
> Again in his
> Own Wake.[46]

The passage calls for an acceptance of history. It evokes images of America (Finn = Huckleberry Finn), of Shakespearean tragedy (tribal and double = Macbeth, the witches' incantation), of Greek myth (wide awake rocks = Odysseus, Scylla, and Charybdis), of James Joyce (fin and wake = Finnegan's Wake). The lines encapsulate themes of death and resurrection. The Finn is not only Huckleberry Finn but also, a few lines later, the fin of a fish. The fish is a symbol of Christ who dies (sinking his fin in his own wake) but also rises (since "Wake" refers to death but also to waking, overcoming sleep or death). "Wake" serves on three levels. It keeps alive the sea imagery of the passage as the fish swims in its own wake. It suggests death, since the deceased are "waked"; and life, since waking is a return from the loss of consciousness. The passage is laden with references to American, English, Greek, Irish, and Christian literature. The wide reading of Merton is obvious in these few lines. The fusion of literature and theology, of ancient myth and contemporary faith, is skillfully achieved.

The passage is symbolically rich in its journey motif. *Adventures of Huckleberry Finn* is perhaps the most representative of American novels. It recounts a river journey that is also a journey of self-discovery. The trip down the river is a flight from society allowing Huckleberry to be alone, to escape the hypocrisy and suffocating affection of other people. Finn and Merton make the same voyage. Merton's travels from Europe to America to Asia, from New York to Kentucky, were an effort to define himself, and to do so on his own terms, without the encroachments of people who threatened him by their dishonesty or demands. His journey is typically American, as we shall have occasion to note later.

The "wide awake rocks" suggest the archetypal Western journey, *The Odyssey*. The point of Odysseus's adventures is homecoming. *The Odyssey* will also figure in Merton's epic poem *The Geography of Lograire*. Merton is Odysseus, who seeks a home but finds it elusive. The journey is perilous for Merton as it was for Odysseus, since he is surrounded by dangers, by "wide awake rocks," by resistance that is sometimes conscious and deliberate.

The lines in question converge in images of death. The *Macbeth* passage recalls the witches, the death prophecy, the specter of mortality that haunts Macbeth. The craft in the stanza is described as "fatal." The protagonist endures "cutlash"; "to kill time" denotes the end of life. The sinking of "his fin" and the "Wake" denote death but also suggest, as we have seen, resurrection.

The ten lines of the stanza describe the life and death journeys of mythic and modern heroes. The history lesson all must learn is the need to accept one's own death in order to conquer the evil of history. The prologue of the poem is dated May 1967. In December 1968 Merton dies.

The images of loneliness in Section 20a are balanced by the images of history and rootedness in Section 20b. But even here there is aloneness, since death is always a singular experience, a singularity that is a key part of the process. The journey to evade it is futile. History cannot be evaded. History tells us that death is not only inevitable but necessary. Death is *the* journey, serving as model and motive for all the others. In Christian myth, the journey leads beyond itself to transcendent homecoming. The journey into death is a pilgrimage to life, to a final, indestructible, deathless life. Ironically, the evasion of death reinforces death. Death encountered is death subdued.

There is a passage in *Cables to the Ace* that is among the most beautiful and personal Merton ever wrote. It is striking in its description of death in a distant country, of Eastern asceticism, and of coming full circle in life. In the year after this poem is finished, Merton dies in a distant country, in search of Eastern mysticism, completing a circle with his life that takes him from secular to sacred to secular, from an interest in the East as a college student to a commitment to the West in monasticism, to a journey to the East as a contemplative. The passage refers to the hermitage and to the longing that is the essence of life. It is Zen-like in its reference to a fathomless "love cry":

> Better to study the germinating waters of my wood
> And know this fever: or die in a distant country
> Having become a pure cone
> Or turn to my eastern abstinence
> With that old inscrutable love cry
> And describe a perfect circle.[47]

As the poem comes to a close, the poet suggests mystery and final resolution:

> I am about to build my nest…
> As I walk away from this poem
> Hiding the ace of freedoms—[48]

We have been discussing the journey of Merton back to his origins. We have dealt with the influence of his mother and of the feminine in his life. It is his father, however, who figures more largely in Merton's career.

At a decisive moment, perhaps the most decisive moment in Merton's life, he experiences his deceased father as alive and with him in his room one night in Rome. He is filled with self-disgust and guilt and begins a conversion experience that will lead him, a decade later, into the Abbey of Gethsemani.

After Ruth Merton dies, Thomas has ten years with his father. When they are together, the time is warm and happy. But Thomas suffers a double loss. His mother is deceased and his father is absent. There are long years in the large, lonely house in New York. His father appears on the scene suddenly, intermittently. He leaves unpredictably. The young Thomas has no parental guarantee that he will be cared for or loved.

But his father remains a powerful influence in his life. When Thomas began his master's thesis at Columbia, he explored, in a study on William Blake, the principles by which his father lived, namely, the idea that aesthetic and spiritual experiences are often interchangeable. His father always liked Blake and read his poetry to his son. Merton's entire adult life is a search for artistic and spiritual excellence, one sustaining the other, both converging into a striking unity, each initiated by his father.

One of the reasons that impels Thomas Merton to enter the Abbey of Gethsemani is the need for a home. We have made references to this theme a number of times throughout this book. When Merton enters the monastery, he is fortunate to find in his first abbot, Frederic Dunne, a remarkably sensitive and fatherly man. There are uncanny coincidences in Dunne's background and in Merton's life. Frederic Dunne came from Zanesville, Ohio, the town where Ruth Jenkins Merton was born. He was attuned to the value of writing and publishing because he came from a family of professional printers. The *Seven Storey Mountain* and *The Sign of Jonas* document abundantly the struggle the young monk undergoes in deciding whether the encouragement he has been given to write is compatible with his Cistercian vocation and his commitment of silence. It is Frederic Dunne who leads him carefully and confidently to achieve the reconciliation. In this, he gives Merton a second birth; he "fathers" him into a life of writing.

One of the sources of Merton's hesitation about writing was not only a fear about whether it could be harmonized with silence but also a fear about his own vanity. Writing involves a certain amount of renown and publicity. Merton had written some anonymous pieces for the abbey, but the major works he now prepares will bear his own name. Dunne's willingness to let this happen enabled Merton to reconcile the consequent ego satisfaction of notoriety with the severe demands of his Trappist vocation.

In an even larger sense, Frederic Dunne played the role of father for the young monk. It is unlikely that Merton would have remained in the monastery had he not developed his talents through writing. Dunne brings Merton to birth both as a monk and as a writer. In Dunne, Merton discovers the lost father. He writes touchingly of Dunne in *The Sign of Jonas*:

> I suppose, since I was the author of the book, I must take responsibility for *The Seven Storey Mountain*. But there was

> one man who was in a certain sense even more responsible for that book...Dom Frederic Dunne, my spiritual Father [who] formed and shaped my whole monastic destiny...Dom Frederic not only "made" me as a writer [but also as a] contemplative... I shall never forget the simplicity and affection with which he put the first copy of the book [*The Seven Storey Mountain*] in my hand. He did not say anything. He just handed me the book, amused at my surprise. But I knew that he was happier about it than I could ever be.[49]

Unfortunately, for yet another time in his life, someone on whom Merton relied is taken by sudden and early death. The next abbot, James Fox, does not see the connection between Merton the monk and Merton the writer.

The search for a father is a frequent theme in *Cables to the Ace.* Three anthems in the poem help to unify it. The first of these occurs in Section 7 and begins "Weep, weep little day"; the second, Section 45, is a prayer to a saint, "Anatole, Anatole"; the third, Section 80, is concerned with Christ: "Slowly, slowly/ comes Christ through the garden." In this final anthem, Christ makes his way slowly through the gardens of Eden, Gethsemani, and Easter, and weeps. The weeping ties the last anthem to the first.

The first anthem sets the tone for the long poem. It is concerned with original sin and Father's Day. The call to "weep, weep" is a summons to sorrow because the Father is lost and no one knows his name. The anthem deals with human origins, with our emergence from apes, with our halting efforts to stand erect and to devise a language. The weeping occurs throughout the anthem, forming a refrain, because we cannot find our Father and connect with our roots. The inability to find our Father and call him by name accounted for our original sin.

In the corresponding anthems, the prayer to Anatole in Section 45 and the description of Christ in Section 80, the need to discover one's origins is developed further. The prayer to Anatole cannot be heard because of noisy jets, riots, wars, fast cars, screeching bombers. The human cry for one's father is muted. It comes from a deep need, but it is no louder than the human voice or the human heart. The clamor made by machines and industry smothers the soft sounds of human desire. We are fathered by the violence of modernity rather than by the tenderness of the human family. Merton's interest in nonviolence is also an interest in restoring the human dimension to the world in which we live.

The subtitle to *Cables to the Ace* is *Familiar Liturgies of Misunderstanding*. The cable is a message to the Ace, or the Father. But the liturgy of modern life, its rituals and frenzy, destroy communication. We have forgotten the name by which God is to be called, the language by which the message we send can be read. The laws of technology have taken the place of the language of the heart.

Christ, nonetheless, comes slowly, slowly through the garden of life. He is encountered in the garden, not in the factory. He is met by those who go slowly rather than by those who travel quickly. He is a Christ who calls us by name, who uses the grammar of the heart, who enchants creation with the words he speaks to it. In the first garden, Eden, Christ speaks to the trees and their branches bear light. In Gethsemane, Christ summons the disciples in his silence, by his sorrow, but they sleep. In the Easter garden, Christ calls those who are lost by their proper names. Both Eden and Easter are beyond history: the trees bear light in Eden and the disciples answer their call, respond to their names, at Easter. Gethsemane is in history. Here the disciples are asleep; the Lord of history weeps.

The two years Thomas Merton lived in New York with his grandparents and without his father were utter misery for him. He learned loneliness in those years, after his mother's death, in a way he never forgot. He was overjoyed when, at the age of seven, he was taken by his father to France. The joy was short-lived. He was placed in a boarding school, a *lycée*, and there experienced a deeper loneliness. He ached for his father and for home. The stress led to a series of illnesses, a pattern followed in Merton's later life, as we have seen.

When Owen Merton began to build a home at Saint-Antonin for his family, Thomas again saw the possibility of happiness. Two trees were planted, one for Thomas, one for John Paul. Every weekend Thomas went home to his father. These were the most meaningful moments of his young life. For a reason Thomas could not fathom, the building of the house was abandoned. Once again the hope for a home was dashed. Now Thomas was in England, again alone. The greatest tragedy of his life befell him. His father developed a brain tumor and died when Thomas was sixteen. After his father's death, Thomas was taken care of by a Harley Street, London physician, Dr. Thomas Bennet.

The hunger in Thomas for affection and meaning, for some permanence, for at least pleasure if happiness were impossible, led him into wild and desperate excesses. He was loud and sometimes shocking in his behavior. At the Oakham boarding school, in England, he drew attention to himself by playing music at top volume and opening the windows in his room to let others know he was there. Nothing could compensate for the loss of his father. He became aggressive and sarcastic, enjoyed shattering what he thought were the illusions by which people lived. Later, at Cambridge, alcohol and sex became new ways to rebel. Eventually, his guardian, Dr. Bennet, could take no more. As a result of a sexual liaison, a child was conceived and his guardian told Thomas he would not continue him at Cambridge or support him in London.

Bennet was a father substitute whom Merton names as one of the people he respected and admired deeply. His guardian gave the young man credit for intelligence and maturity, a confidence Merton sorely needed. When Dr. Bennet could abide Merton no longer, the loneliness and insecurity returned even more painfully. Merton was damaged and permanently scarred by his losses.

Of the many scenes *The Seven Storey Mountain* describes, few are more disturbing than that in which Thomas receives a telegram from his dying father. The telegram is incoherent, a startling indication of his father's loss of consciousness and memory. Thomas is alone in a large house when he reads it. He was alone under a tree when he read of his mother's imminent death. Later, again by telegram, he will learn of John Paul's death. Later, by cable, the Abbey of Gethsemani will learn of Thomas's death. Cables, letters, messages of death. When Thomas reads his father's message, he knows death is inevitable. The terror is intensified by the fact that there is no one with whom he can share it.

Toward the end of his own life, Merton returns to the thoughts of the lost father. We have seen some of these references in *Cables to the Ace.* His conversion begins when he senses his father's presence after death. As his life draws to a close, he searches again for that presence. His father has something to do with his artistic temperament, with the development of a religious instinct in him, with the conversion experience that begins his vocation, with the search for home and father culminating in Gethsemani, with the later poetry, and with an emptiness in him nothing could satisfy.

John Paul

The first time Thomas Merton expresses the tenderness he feels toward his younger brother, John Paul, is in the poem he writes when he receives word of his brother's death. The poem is one of his finest.

Poetry emerges from the unconscious with its symbols, metaphors, and images. Deep in the psyche of Thomas Merton the affection he feels for his brother surfaces. The affection is so deep and the personal dimensions of the emotions so strong that even the opening words do not cloy as in other instances they might have. "Sweet brother," he writes in his autobiography. And the words are right. They capture the innocence and youth of the slain brother, the heartache and hurt of the surviving poet. Merton recalls in *The Seven Storey Mountain* the serene nature of John Paul, free from the complex drives and obsessions of Thomas. He remembers the constant happiness of his younger brother, hears in his memory the tune, always the same tune, his infant brother sang each night in his crib.

The poem is dominated by references to homelessness. John Paul had also been deprived of a home. Merton became acutely aware of this as he reflects on his younger brother's burial at sea. To be lost in the vast ocean seems somehow a more total loss. No marker is possible, no return to the place of burial warranted. The poem ends with a plea to his brother to find a home at last since he found none in this world.

Throughout the poem, the poet wishes to take his brother's place. He asks that his own experiences become a vicarious form of relief for his brother. Eventually the poet turns to Christ, the third and eldest brother of the poem, in the hope that healing be granted John Paul by Christ since Thomas is not adequate to the task. Christ, the unknown brother for many years, is asked to make the two brothers known to each other and to bring them to life.

John Paul does not figure largely in *The Seven Storey Mountain.* The references to him are few and are related as isolated instances rather than connected with a larger scheme of meaning. The intensity of the references when they occur, however, is remarkable. We are led to suspect that there are subterranean depths in the brotherly relationship that were never fully explored.

In John Paul, Thomas was dealing not only with his brother but with the entire human race. When one realizes this, one is less surprised by the direction the later thinking of Thomas Merton assumes. Many of his readers were shocked by the strong social protest he registered in the 1960s. Some of this, of course, was always with him. From the influence of his pacifist mother to his involvement with socialism and communism at Columbia to his work in Harlem one can follow the thread of a constant theme.

The death of his brother and the resultant guilt acted as a catalyst for the writings of the last decade of his life. It takes Merton a long time to find this new medium of protest and to convince himself it is legitimate. He had to work through his Cistercian and contemplative vocation and the reconciliation of these with a career in writing. He required the influence of the Second Vatican Council to validate for himself personally, and even for his religious community, engagement in social issues. He had already proved himself unconventional by blending a Trappist vocation and a career in writing. He is all the more a maverick by uniting a Cistercian commitment with a social critique of the world. He settles these questions for himself while working on a journal entitled *Conjectures of a Guilty Bystander.*

In the racial and peace issues that preoccupy the closing years of his life, Merton makes an effort to achieve unity in himself as well as to overcome the divisions that separate people. The unity in himself requires a deeper relationship with the world that he had apparently abandoned in disgust. In a sense, the world is his cross and his salvation. He had seen it as the adversary when he entered the monastery. It now becomes the arena in which universal relationships are to be achieved. He had made peace with God. It is now time to make peace with the human family, a family that becomes more real to him than the family he had lost in three tragic deaths.

The bridge from the death of John Paul to the recovery of a larger family of brothers and sisters in the 1960s was provided by Mahatma Gandhi. Gandhi taught Merton about secular grace, so to speak, about the discovery of the religious in the political realm, and more important, about the achievement of the encounter between God and humanity in the context of a world order. Gandhi writes:

> I could not lead a religious life unless I identified myself with the whole of mankind, and that I could not do unless I took part in politics. The whole gamut of man's activities today constitutes an indivisible whole. You cannot divide social, economic, political, and purely religious work into watertight compartments.[50]

In *The Geography of Lograire*, the Cain-Abel myth becomes one of the dominant themes of the poem. It is a journey the poet makes to his beginnings at the very end of his life. The Cain-Abel myth assumes the importance that it does because of the troubled character of the Thomas-John Paul relationship. For Merton, the Fall, the essence of original sin, is realized in the neglect of the brother. The final poems seek to overcome our indifference and hostility toward one another. *Cables to the Ace* is an effort to come to terms with our inertia, to get beyond the noise and the chatter to the heart of the matter and to the meaning between us. *The Geography of Lograire* seeks to get us to lay down arms, to affirm relationship so strongly that nonviolence becomes the hallmark of our encounters. Behind these last great poems of Thomas Merton, one senses the figure of John Paul and the loss of the only brother life gave him.

We shall have occasion to discuss *The Geography of Lograire* in considerable detail in the next chapter. It is useful now to recall a few themes from the prologue to the poem, which sets the mood for the epic and which evokes images of lost brotherhood and the lost father.

The poem opens with a white slave captain seeking a black runaway along the rivers of the South. The rivers of the world carry death rather than life. They allow the merchants of slavery to continue their system. The waters run with the blood of rejected relationships rather than with refreshment and renewal. Brother seeks to destroy brother with little thought of the common history and deep meaning that destine them for each other. The chains of slavery are the substitute a mistaken world makes for the bonds of family. The prologue summons before us not only the Cain-Abel myth but the David-Absalom, father-son, story as well. We are reminded of the voyage of Odysseus and his ten-year effort to reach homeland and son, wife and family.

The prologue then turns to the journey of Abraham. It is a journey that becomes symbolic for the religious search that leads to a heavenly Father and a celestial home. And now the religious themes cluster. The sin of Cain is mentioned explicitly, as well as the Brother who comes not with weapons in his hands but with Redemption. The journey of Abraham, like the sin of Cain before it, leads to Christ. Adam's failure as father of the race creates the possibility for Cain's betrayal of brotherhood and Christ's restoration of it. The father's sin descends on the son; Christ heals all relationships by canceling the Fall and becoming its victim.

In Merton's vision, we are bound not by the disobedience of Adam, nor by the anger of Cain, nor by the innocent blood of Abel that cries out for vengeance. We are bound by Christ, whose life stirs in all of us. And Christ is bound to the Father by sonship, to us by brotherhood.

In Christ the journey of Abraham, the fall of Adam, the failure of Cain reach a point of resolution. Cain's name is changed to "pain" and the chant of "Pain and Abel" end this sober prologue. Christ absorbs the pain and the evil.

Merton's life was influenced, as we have seen, by the tragedies and losses in his own family. In his Columbia days, he comes under the influence of a few professors who give him a sense of stability amid the turbulence of his own emotional life. The poet Mark Van Doren and the philosopher Dan Walsh provide inspiration and guidance. They are father figures for him in the years between the death of his own father and the father he finds in the Abbey of Gethsemani. During the Columbia days he reaches out for friends who become a lifelong family for him. Chief among these are Robert Lax and Edward Rice. They become brothers in an extended family. Later, the candor in his journals will amount to a plea that he be accepted, a petition that his readers accept him as their brother.

The pain of the journey became a catalyst for Merton's creativity. The restlessness and the contradictions made him dissatisfied with himself. But happiness and contentment are not the same. He became happy when he no longer demanded happiness for himself. He found happiness the moment he stopped looking for it.

CHAPTER SIX

Cargo Cults and Ghost Dances

Among the most subtle of our influences are the myths by which we live. When the myths are creative they energize us with life. When they are negative, they move us in the direction of self-destruction.

The century in which Merton lived was dominated by cultures carefully organized, heavily industrialized, supposedly rational. The myth of the rationality of the modern world is so pervasive that most believe there are no myths driving it. Myth is viewed as the opposite of reason. Cultures less well educated and less economically effective are deemed more prone to myth. The most foolish of myths is the myth that there are cultures not driven by myths.

Merton defined myth as an imaginative synthesis of facts and intuitions. One has a certain amount of hard evidence and a certain amount of intuitive experience about reality. One accounts for the unity of the human family, for example, by the Adam and Eve myth. Facts suggest the human race is bound by radical and unalterable similarities, and intuition affirms this with conviction. Many cultures have developed contrary myths about the supposed superiority of one human group over another, a superiority allegedly deriving from human nature itself.

Once we accept the myth of a unified family we deal with people differently. The myth becomes part of our meaning system and worldview. It acts as a norm for judgment and behavior. It shapes character and determines the influence we have upon others. It is a powerful and persuasive force in human history as a whole and in individual lives as such.

Original Child Bomb

In a telling prose poem entitled *Original Child Bomb*, Merton explored the myths at the core of our attitude toward war. The poem deals with the detonation of the first atomic bomb over Hiroshima. The "child" delivered to Japan is the fruit of an efficient, technological society that not only creates ingenious products but delivers them to their destination unerringly. "Original Child Bomb" is the name the Japanese give to the nuclear weapon unleashed against them. The weapon is seen by Americans as life-giving since it will save lives. It is seen by the Japanese as an instrument of death. The "child" is alive only as long as it kills. Americans, operating with a different myth, are proud of their "child"; the Japanese are reduced by this "new life" to terror and despair.

The poem is a series of dates, a record of documents, a gathering of data. It holds its meaning behind the bland recital of facts under enormous pressure. Statistics and reports are so arranged that a tension is set up among them. A rhythm is established by juxtaposition. It builds to a climax both horrible to the imagination and liberating for the emotions. The poem is a brilliant tour de force worthy of Ernest Hemingway in its capacity to keep language to its most simple expression and yet charge it with almost unbearable meaning.

The approach Thomas Merton uses is perfect for the subject of the poem. Atomic holocaust so devastates the imagination that it does not lend itself to florid description. An unemotional reportorial style captures the essence of nuclear brutality in the only way the mind can handle it.

The work is poetic in its ability to suggest infinitely more than it says. It is dramatic in the tension it generates and in the conflicts it portrays.

The drama is intensified by the visual quality of the scenes and incidents it depicts.

The subtitle of the book reads: *Points for Meditation to Be Scratched on the Walls of a Cave.* It is a meditation indeed. The book serves as an important document, furthermore, in a strategy of nonviolence although those words are not used in the poem. The starkness of the text is complemented by spare drawings. They frame the nightmare without overburdening it. They suggest by their unrefined character the scratchings on the wall of a cave.

Many Americans saw in this "child" the possibility of eternal peace. In this, it became an object of faith. The bomb became also an object of necessity once America accepted the myth that surrender from an enemy must be a total, unconditional surrender. Such "peace" terms are the substance of further belligerence, an act of aggression against the vulnerable and the defeated. Once the myth of absolute surrender is granted, no horror to bring it about is deemed excessive. When one lives in a culture that defines good and evil in terms that are not nuanced, total victory becomes necessary in every contest one enters. A concession to the other is deemed a compromise with evil. A more human dimension of compassion in surrender dulls, it is believed, the luster of triumph. In the American cowboy myth, victory is always clean, undiluted, decisive. The vanquished must be defeated in a manner that will not permit their return.

The idea of exploding the bomb over Kyoto, a city rich in Japanese history and tradition, is rejected because this might cause too much bitterness and criticism throughout the world. Tokyo was spared because it had already been fire-bombed in one of the most savage attacks ever made on a city in ancient or modern warfare. Hiroshima won out in the discussions. Lucky Hiroshima, Merton observes. Westerners knew of

Tokyo and Kyoto, but Hiroshima was unknown. Now it would be made famous. All the world would know of Hiroshima.

Merton weaves into the account the language of the Christian myth that was used by America in the process of creating and delivering this "child." An atomic device had recently been exploded in New Mexico. The name for the device was "Trinity." "Trinity" was successful. In a parody of the beatific vision, it illuminated the entire landscape. The light was so bright that it could cause blindness. It was a light that was also darkness. In mystic theology, God is described in such terms. An official who witnesses the explosion and is overwhelmed by the brightness and seemingly omnipotent power before him cries out: "Lord, I believe. Help thou my unbelief."

Admiral Leahy was a "doubting Thomas." He thought the bomb would not explode. Others had faith in the bomb. They would remember his doubt and count it weakness. War cannot be waged successfully by those who doubt the possibility of miracles. Wars are made for true believers.

Winston Churchill is told of the successful experiment with the code message: "Babies satisfactorily born."[51] It is nativity time in the tides of war. An original child, a Christmas savior, is about to be born. The "child" will usher in an era of peace. And the light that will guide us will exceed that of the star that marked the birth of Jesus.

The myth of efficiency and of technological wizardry was entering into its most awesome manifestation. The *U.S.S. Indianapolis* leaves San Francisco, the city named after the poor man of Assisi who once sang songs to Brother Sun, Sister Moon. A greater light is now in the making. The ship contains U-235 in a lead bucket, the material needed to bring the bomb to life over its target. The destination of the *Indianapolis* is Tinian Island; instructions stipulate that, should the ship sink, the uranium is to be saved before any lives. In cultures fueled by the industrial myth, human beings often accompany and serve the larger reality of the artifact or product, the machine or assembly line. Such servants may be asked to surrender their lives if the idol is endangered.

Themes of life and death exchange places in a death dance. There is more than parody in the scene. There is also pageantry. The myth has become ritual. Colonel Paul Tibbets, in command of the B-29 that will deliver the "child" safely, baptizes his airplane the *Enola Gay* in honor of his mother, who lives in Iowa. The plane that carries the "child" achieves motherhood. The bomb is assembled on Tinian. Those who create it refer to it as a "little boy" and handle it with respect and tenderness. On a Sunday afternoon, a day for traditional Christian veneration, the "little boy" is borne in procession and enfolded in the womb of *Enola Gay.*

The delivery is successful. Seventy thousand people are killed immediately or die in a few hours. A communiqué observes that the visible effects of the fireball exceed "Trinity." The *Enola Gay* reports that it is now heading for "Papacy." "Papacy" is the code name for the island of Tinian.

On August 9, 1945, another bomb is dropped on Nagasaki while Hiroshima still burns.

In September of 1963, Nobel laureate Linus Pauling wrote a letter commending Merton's poem. He detects only one error in the poem. The Hiroshima fireball was 1,800 feet across, not 18,000 feet, as the text of the poem reports.

Zen and the Art of Engineering

Engineering is a myth the modern world accepts. The myth assumes that life can be managed by problem-solving techniques. The myth has an element of truth to it, as do most myths. The difference between the element of truth and the rest of the myth, in this case, amounts to obsession. The myth supposes that all of life can be controlled and reduced to rational regulation. We become impatient with others and even with ourselves when people do not fit comfortably into whatever prearranged plan we are pursuing. People become an obstacle when their humanity and emotions get in the way.

In his book *Zen and the Birds of Appetite*, Merton quotes Herbert Marcuse's idea that the rationality and exactitude of technological society with all its attendant justifications amount to a new form of mystification. Zen offers a helpful antidote since it draws our attention and concern to that which *is*. It helps us yield to the world rather than fit the world into our plans for it. Zen stresses pure consciousness rather than consciousness *of* or *about* something or someone.

The tendency in the West is to transform reality into our image; the tendency in Zen is to accept reality as it is or to be transformed into it. In the West, control is prized. A multitude of human values issue from this approach, it is true, but control can become obsessive when not balanced by resiliency and mysticism.

The least pragmatic of alternatives is ironically and paradoxically the most practical at times. Nothing seems less efficient to the modern world than contemplation. But contemplation reduces our obsessions so that we go about life with greater freedom. Time given to prayer may appear as wasted time in a busy schedule. But such time can enable us to relate to time in a more humanly productive manner. We must, however, avoid the Western need to make contemplation another tool in the control of life. The practical benefits of contemplation should not be sought, merely accepted. There are functional advantages to love and friendship also, but they retard or destroy a relationship when they are pursued for their own sake.

Zen offers relief from the inordinate and paralyzing self-consciousness of the West. The reduction of reality to the self creates anxiety, since the self is not capable of encompassing reality. Reality is a process, not a product. It slips through our fingers if we try to clutch it.

Zen is not the final solution to the human dilemma. The West also has insights worth preserving. But Zen is especially attuned to those deficiencies and obsessions in the West that are most perilous. Nothing gives all the answers. Indeed, a world in which we had all the answers would be a world in which God had no life, Merton observes. Answers become system oriented and harden easily into dogma and orthodoxy. Questions keep the world open and encourage infinite possibilities and endless activity.

The effort to control has as its driving force a desire for affluence, for power, for prestige. In all three instances, the self is exalted. Such a world is kept at an intolerable pitch of tension, made eager always for "more," kept restless with the fact that there is never enough. Ironically, the system that exalts the self is terrified of the self. It seeks to protect the self in a fortress of power and prestige, indulgence and acquisitions. The result is a social structure outwardly ordered and sane, inwardly turbulent with compulsion, delusions, and greed. Within the structure, we succumb to the Faustian temptation to create a meaning that is ours alone and to do this in competition with and ultimately in isolation from others.

Organized affluence often masks human despair. People are seldom more grim than when they are in the process of moneymaking. Fiscal responsibility too readily is equated with maturity. Caring for others is deemed less astute than caring for one's own finances. The myth of affluence makes it difficult for us to see that little of substance is achieved in affluence. It is merely a highly organized approach to superficiality. Merton's *Faith and Violence* and *Seeds of Destruction* explore these ideas.

Affluence is concerned with the surface, not the reality, with how one looks rather than with how one is, with what one owns rather than with what one has become. It is the least serious of human endeavors, pursued with a gravity that verges on comedy since excessive attention is given to a matter of little human consequence. We do not laugh because the myth and ritual of moneymaking have made us imagine that abundant life is at issue in our gross earning power.

Merton criticized the motives and the results that derive from a preoccupation with control. The control myth generates the progress myth. As quantitative control is established over matter and nature, we assume that our lives are enriched qualitatively. The myth of progress depends upon major improvement in areas of life that are not substantive. It requires the subjugation of nature, indeed, human nature, to the agenda of affluence and advancement.

The nonsubstantive areas of our lives are those most easily managed and quantified. Values such as faith or love cannot be controlled or measured. Substantive failures such as selfishness or greed cannot be eliminated from human life by "progress." The nonsubstantive issues, however, are subject to improvement and easily beguile us with the notion that we have made human progress when we have merely enhanced human comfort. Loneliness is not canceled out by radio, television, jet travel, print or social media, Internet or mobile phones. The mystery of suffering and the terror of death are not eliminated by a superb medical system or by extensive counseling and careful research. No matter how birth is monitored it remains an astounding event that shatters our rational categories.

The management of progress in nonsubstantive areas of life is attested to by bureaucracies. Merton was not always balanced in his critique of bureaucracy. The necessity of bureaucracy and the nobility of some people involved in the system escaped his notice. When dealing with bureaucratic excess, however, Merton could be incisive.

The bureaucratic tendency to control nonsubstantive areas of life leads to a society that celebrates pseudo-events. In such "events" our favorite group myths are celebrated. Progress in a new weapons system is reported as providing us with personal security. Improvement in the economy indicates that a benign fiscal providence will guide us in the coming years as tenderly and surely as God once did. Household products are heralded as an advance in marital happiness. We become sanctified as we play the ritual game of contributing to the gross national product. To be gainfully employed is to be judged humanly worthwhile. The atomic bombing of Hiroshima is an apt example of how we can focus on the wizardry of the weapon or the requirements of the ritual that deliver it or the making of a myth necessitating unconditional surrender. In all this, the essential fact of human destruction is neglected or accepted joyfully. The accuracy and the complexity of the achievement make us marvel at the intelligence, the progress, the efficiency of it all.

Merton is broadly insightful in his analysis. He does not, however, balance thinking with nuance and further refinement. His prophetic proclamation style overlooks the values economic structures and science contribute to human life. His point is well-taken but other points need to be made.

The pursuit of money has become for a large number of people the great modern romance. The grail of contemporary life is gold.

> ...the ritual that surrounds money transactions, the whole liturgy of marketing and of profit, is basically void of reality and of meaning. Yet we treat it as the final reality, the absolute meaning, in the light of which everything else is to be judged...[52]

Merton believed that the myth of control, certitude, affluence will eventually be undermined by two powerful forces in the West: the new physics and the turn, in religious matters, to the East. When Merton read Heisenberg's *Physics and Philosophy*, he was intrigued with the author's uncertainty principle. Heisenberg concluded that the ultimate constitution of matter was so elusive that in logical terms nothing existed at the core of matter. In its radical expression, matter had no form. Heisenberg's insights were in accord with the insights of Zen Buddhism.

Heisenberg, however, was a great physicist. Westerners would be more influenced by science than by contemplation. The West could be led to the East by the very science the West saw as the direct opposite of Asian mysticism. In Zen, nonexistence is considered a way of existing. Reality is somehow beyond both existence and nonexistence. In Heisenberg's work, the universe is held together by the mysterious and inevitable interaction of all the differing parts. Even the elements in the system that seem contradictory somehow contribute. Later, physics would discover black holes and antimatter as essential to the structure by which illuminated bodies and matter itself survived. The universe is a carnival of opposites and contradictions.

Merton believed that in Heisenberg and in Albert Einstein the myth of materialism and certitude was exposed for what it was. The myth was built not on science or knowledge, as it was supposed, but on a naïve faith. Nineteenth-century science and religion clashed partly because they were competing faiths. Contemporary science is less hostile to religion because it is more tentative in its assertions. Correlatively, nineteenth-century religion tended to see itself as a science with categories of certitude, infallibility, and inflexible dogma. Newman, with his convergence-of-probabilities theory, and Merton, with his dialectical approach to the truth, were examples of how enlightened religious thinkers moved into a more nuanced definition of faith. Science and religion came to appreciate the myths that motivated both areas of human understanding.

Toward the end of his life, Merton attacked the hunger for certitude and control which characterized the Church at large and lessened its influence. The myth of certitude on one side creates a demand for blind obedience on the other. This obedience may be pressed so relentlessly that it amounts to a renunciation of human rights, human needs, human feelings, human conscience. A need to dominate others may compensate in some cases for the loss of family life. In *Disputed Questions*, Merton speaks of this tendency when celibacy and institution become myths.

Merton's most painful asceticism was not the rigor of Cistercian life, about which he does not complain, but the sacrifice of pursuing creative alternatives while remaining in an institution that did not always favor this. In this decision, his dialectical approach to life is again evident. He was a man who saw the need for legitimate authority in the world at large, in the Church more specifically, in his personal life most particularly. But he was also a person who felt called to develop his charisms and conscience, his personal talents and prophetic insights, his artistic creativity and intellectual interests. He was overjoyed when he was finally able to become a hermit because he was allowed maximum time for himself but also subjected in a broad way to the structure of a monastic community and of an authority larger than his own judgment. Life would have been easier in blind obedience or belligerent anarchy. He chose a path between both.

The myth of pragmatic individualism did not appeal to him. For Merton, Robinson Crusoe was a manifestation of the Western myth that we can control all the elements of our lives in isolation from others.

He wanted to be a hermit, not Robinson Crusoe. He did not wish to be alone, to think alone, to choose alone.

The Legend of Tucker Caliban

The latter years of Thomas Merton's life were marked by a growing interest in myths. As we shall see, legends, such as that of Tucker Caliban, historical myths, such as cargo cults and ghost dances, and the rituals of Native Americans and Latin Americans fascinated him. In the background of this interest there were shadows of Zen Buddhism and Mahatma Gandhi, of medieval Cistercian monasticism and modern poetry. In *The Geography of Lograire*, he would make an effort to bring it all together.

The Tucker Caliban legend was developed as a parable by William Melvin Kelley in his book *A Different Drummer*. Merton had been led to Kelley's book because of his deepening interest in black culture. He was convinced, for example, that spirituals represented a more creative form of liturgical music than that developed by trained professionals, monks in libraries, and curial officials. Black music came out of the torment and tension of life. It was, therefore, more suitable for worship. Liturgical music registers most strongly, Merton observed, when people suffer oppression and have their lives robbed of identity. From this, there is born a hunger for freedom, a yearning for truth and meaning that is profoundly religious and deeply human.

The interest in such music led Merton to read black writers. He was impressed with the raw vitality of Richard Wright and the eschatological and apocalyptic dimension of James Baldwin's *The Fire Next Time* and *Go Tell It on the Mountain*. In William Melvin Kelley's book, however, he believed that he had discovered a singularly prophetic and richly mythic black novel. The book was a parable that caught the spiritual implications of the black struggle and created from it a morality play.

The action of the drama is built around a hegira from the South.

The Tucker Caliban legend is a story dealing with American myths of race, commerce, and violence. As the narrative begins, a group of idle white men watch as a large shipment of rock salt is made ready for delivery to the farm of a black man, Tucker Caliban. (The name Caliban, of course, suggests the slave in William Shakespeare's *Tempest.*) Although the group appears indifferent, the forces of prejudice and hatred are boiling within them. They will be idle only until these forces reach that mysterious level of intensity where personal confusion and self-hate are transformed into violence and fury. At that moment, they will become not a circle of observers but a lynch mob, galvanized into action by a myth they believe in more deeply than their own humanity.

The myth of violence in American culture is often exemplified by a supposed triumph of absolute goodness over an allegedly thoroughly evil adversary. In the nineteenth century, the myth is enacted with cowboys and Indians. The twentieth-century re-creation of the saga continues the melodrama with whites and blacks, capitalists and communists. Later, the myth assumes cosmic proportions. It is played out, Merton observes, with hydrogen bombs, Polaris submarines, and intercontinental ballistic missiles.

In the Tucker Caliban parable, Tucker is a mythic figure, descendant of a great African chief. He has been diminished in American society so that his physical stature is diminutive, his emotional life intense rather than expressive, his manner taciturn rather than articulate. Tucker has purchased rock salt to sterilize his farm so that no life can grow there again. He shoots his mule and cow, burns his house to the ground, ravages the earth, and leaves in the night with his pregnant wife. No life should come to the light of day in this bedeviled region of the earth. Tucker Caliban vanishes and is never heard from again.

Caliban's action becomes contagious, his spirit active even in his absence. All the blacks suddenly abandon the South, the doors of their homes left ajar, the furniture forsaken. They obey an inner call to flee and to leave their native region a wasteland. None of the whites knows where they go.

Rev. Bennett Bradshaw, a northern black leader who founds a community called the Black Jesuits, hears the story of Tucker Caliban and comes South to learn its meaning. He is an outsider to the black community, a northerner in the South, a cultural and religious opportunist. He arrives on the scene, not to identify with his people, nor to justify their hegira, but to learn from the situation so as to gain personally from it.

A circle of idle white men observes the arrival of Bradshaw. They convince themselves that Bradshaw is responsible for the exodus of the blacks. Confused and angered by events, they seek a scapegoat to make life more bearable, a vicarious object on whom to vent their rage. The fact that Bradshaw is black and a northerner allows them to find in him an adversary who threatens them on two different counts.

Bradshaw is beaten and driven in his own Cadillac to the gutted Caliban farm. The myth now functions on two levels, racial and commercial. The Cadillac has become a symbol of success in the American myth of affluence. The fact that a black owns an automobile the whites cannot afford seals his fate. The myth is also regional in its conflict between North and South. It reenacts, furthermore, the biblical myth of Cain and Abel and the national myth of the Civil War.

The parable ends with the screams of Bradshaw as he is tortured and made ready for hanging. His pleas for life cannot be heard by the blacks who have deserted; the whites who hear the cries are incited by them to inflict death more painfully. The circle of men becomes a circle of death. They execute Bradshaw but are brutalized by their own obsessions, abandoned to their inner demons with no hope of freedom from them.

Cargo Cults

We have seen how deeply Thomas Merton felt the upheaval of the modern world in his own personal life. This led him to search out some of the sources of that upheaval in the realm of dreams and of the unconscious. We explored in the last chapter the dreams and the unconscious dynamisms that might account for Merton's later theology and behavior. In this chapter we are exploring the cosmic dreams and myths, the global unconscious that may explain the forces at work in the modern world.

Cargo cults exemplify a disturbed religious consciousness.[53] The cults are developed in a culture remote from our own geographically and technologically. Yet somehow they are nearer to us than we first imagine. The cults develop as commerce becomes confused with religion, as materialism is sought in a vain effort to satisfy the craving of the human heart. They are part of an unconscious dream world, a myth system that chooses vulnerable symbols and perishable objects for an imperishable need and an immaterial goal.

Deep in the jungles of New Guinea, a group of men, none of them white, surrounds a landing field built by the great white race. In the daylight, they sing and dance and pass among themselves pieces of paper stolen from the whites. In the darkness, by firelight, they wait. They enact an advent ritual of petition and expectation for a reason that eludes the casual observer.

The natives have seen the great white men sign papers and stamp them with markers. Soon after this ritual, planes bearing cargo or ships with magic products arrive on the scene. Out of the skies or from far beyond the horizon, God sends powerful artifacts as a sign of love and blessing on the whites, as a means by which the whites will remain a privileged race on the earth.

The natives reason that the papers have something to do with God's favor. To a point, they are correct. The superiority of the whites, they believe, does not derive from an inherited greatness but from a knowledge of how to control the resources of the earth. It is all a question of knowing the procedure, of learning the code that would unravel the mystery of communication with God. The problem is not God, who loves all, but knowing the way to reach God.

The natives wait for long hours, sometimes days and weeks. But the planes do not come; the ships never anchor. Something is wrong. When repetition of the ritual brings no response, the cults collapse. But they are revived whenever a charismatic leader appears to promise the natives that a solution is near, that the white race's magic with the papers can at long last be understood.

For Merton, the idea of reading history rationally was a myth. The lines from past to present to future are not forged logically but by means of myths and dreams. These function close to the level of needs and hopes, a level at which reason has little force. We are the subjects and objects of myth dreams.

The New Guinea cargo cults seem naïve. Myth, however, is equally forceful in our own culture. It is difficult to recognize as myth the imperatives that drive a culture. One must achieve a certain distance from a culture in order to demythologize it.

In the United States, money and status allow some to suppose themselves superior to others. Money and status, however, are not more rational in the United States than conch shells and tribal shamen are in other cultures. Money and status are frequently the arbitrary result of the way we handle paper, stamp marks on it, menace an opponent, or resort to gambling and chance. Checks and stocks, certificates and bonds are shuffled in some magical fashion to create power. The winners in the shuffle are victorious, in most cases, because of luck. Paper is exchanged in an arcane and secretive manner. Participants await a response by observing the market or sitting in front of a computer.

Cargo cults derive from a myth that seeks to understand the way the world functions. The myth is fashioned because the natives, like all human beings, are uncertain about the laws governing reality. In its own terms, the cargo cult myth is as sophisticated as any other myth.

In the beginning, it is said, there were two brothers, one of whom unintentionally violated a tribal taboo by killing a forbidden fish. The forbidden fish is another version of the forbidden fruit the West is familiar with in the Judeo-Christian myth of the Fall.

The result of the accident is the separation of the two brothers. The brother who kills the fish is punished and kept, together with his descendants, in a primitive culture. The other brother prospers in a land far away, beyond the ocean. The myth is an amalgam of the creation and the Cain-Abel myth. It seeks to explain the origin of the human family and the reason for its tragic, even homicidal, tendencies. The natives surmised that their lack of cargo, and, consequently, of power or worth in the world, had something to do with an ancestral sin. The cargo myth translated the Fall into the Cain-Able myth.

Cargo cults develop, as we have seen, in an effort to explain the difference between colonialists and natives, between rich and poor. The myth assumes the human family is one and equal. Accidental circumstances, not essential distinctions, account for the dominance of one culture and the enslavement of the other.

The myth fascinates Merton because it has something to do with the fraternal problem that beset him in his personal life, and in his professional life with civil rights and the peace movement. It also intrigues him because of the obvious parallels with biblical, Judeo-Christian mythology.

The native New Guinea cult deals with a sense of inferiority before the white race and with the lingering sense of guilt this instills. The cult is an effort by the oppressed to convince themselves that there is no reason to be guilty about not being white or to feel remorse about being poor. The cargo the white race controls belongs, in some way, to all people. The cultists seek the cargo so that they, too, may be blessed and become brothers and sisters in the equality creation once intended.

At the heart of the cargo ritual is a need to obtain money and material without the enslavement of the self to the white race. In Marxist terms, there is a desire to get beyond the alienation of the work the natives do, work that ensures submission for the natives and profit for their employers. The myth dream of the West derives from a notion of nonreciprocity with people who are not white. The dream has as its content superiority over all others.

There is a further dimension of the cargo myth that parallels modern consciousness, namely, an anxiety for innovation. The New Guinea natives are shocked to discover that their old ways of doing things do not bring them cargo. In a myth system that equates divine favor and material possessions or human relationship and commercial products, the old ways do not work. To be blessed by God, one must possess; to be accepted by others, one must dominate. Salvation requires a new religion; human dignity demands a different liturgy. Change becomes imperative for survival.

In America, the same myth functions although it is ritualized differently. Cargo gives security, convinces people they are worthwhile, saves them as responsible and contributing members of the human family. The old ways are easily surrendered whenever they do not bring cargo, material success, social acceptance. Advertising conjures up myth dreams of paradise, of a better life, of endless possessions. It amounts to a cult, a ritual, full of magic and fantasy, inviting us into the new religion of commerce and cargo, offering a world in which cravings are gratified and wishes become real.

In Merton's view, one of the most persistent fears in the American myth dream is the fear of obsolescence. We discard clothes or houses, automobiles or products, not when they no longer function, but when they no longer fascinate. When the enchantment of our neighbors with our cargo ceases, the dream ends, the magic vanishes. In an effort to restore the illusion we repeat the ritual of moneymaking or impulse buying even though we possess more than we need. The ritual becomes its own end. Liturgy takes the place of God.

In this mindset, the new acquisitions become burdens but we repeat the cycle of gathering in the hope that among the objects we own we may find God or life, happiness or favor with others. When the myth dream is proclaimed in the mass media we become convinced that the compulsion for cargo is the normal way to live, that the illusion of affluence is the same as reality. We dream godlike dreams of omnipotence in which neighbors worship us, become humble before us and respectful of our dignity.

At the heart of the New Guinea myth dream, there is a desire that all human beings be equal. The necessities and luxuries are due to all simply because they are human. The Western myth dream differs in the sense that some should have all, and others, nothing. There is a fear of equality in the white cargo cult.

The fear of equality extends itself to religious matters. The Western religious declare themselves superior to those of the East. Asian religions have little or no concern with proclaiming themselves the only true way. Formal religious life, even monasticism, in the West, is sometimes promoted as a superior lifestyle. God is presented as favoring some who belong to a supposed superior caste, whether it be episcopacy or papacy, ministry or monasticism, Catholicism or Christianity, celibacy or clericalism. Those not included in the caste are seen as remote from God's design or care. They suffer from a lesser insight into truth.

Racism is the result of the fear of inequality. It is important in racism to declare the subjected race less human than the favored race. It is also crucial to deprive the vilified race of cargo and to keep it far from the sources of power or money. Racism encourages us to invite into the ritual and the myth dream only those whose race is the same as our own. Few things enrage a racist more than the affluence of a supposed inferior race. The wealth of the outsider is an affront to the "theology" of racism. Cargo belongs, according to this doctrine, only to those God favors. The intruder is viewed as a heretic, a disturber of the cosmic order, a demon, a renegade. Violence is justified against an insolent race so that the order intended by God might be restored.

When the myth dream is racist, paranoia emerges as a crucial ingredient. Law and order become a magisterium by which orthodoxy is preserved. Inquisitions and censorship, denunciations and threats are standard procedure. The aliens are excommunicated from meaningful association with the allegedly superior race.

The cargo cult phenomenon in its myriad manifestations is a sign of the universal crisis in communication in the modern world. We have lost contact not only with one another but with our own inner depths. At a sufficiently profound level of our psyche, we do not want the cargo, the cult, the affluence, the frenzy. We wish only to be at peace with ourselves and to be accepted as worthwhile by others. Contemplation might put us in touch with those elements in our lives, Merton reasoned, that are most enduring. It would help us exist as real selves, to get beneath the shadow and the disguise, the role playing and the anxiety. Compassion is the fruit of contemplation. In compassion, we might become, not those who drive others to further extremes, but ministers of grace in a world terrified by a myth dream become a nightmare. The nightmare portrays us as competitors who gain only if others lose.

The Geography of Lograire

It was not the kind of poem one would have expected from Thomas Merton. He was, of course, no longer a young poet or an inexperienced monk. There had been changes in his life, some of them quite profound. His prose never registered the changes as radically as did his poetry. His poetry was often the barometer of his soul. In the younger days, it was lyrical and free; in the middle years, passionate and confrontative; at the end, cosmic and visionary.

The final book of poetry took the entire world into its compass. Its sections were entitled "North," "South," "East," and "West." The vertical and horizontal directions formed a cross over the world; the sweep of the action left nothing out of its sphere.

The Geography of Lograire is crucial for an interpretation of Merton's life and thought. It complements the *Seven Storey Mountain* but also supersedes it in its sophistication and universality. It is the most candid of his published works. All of Thomas Merton is there.

The poem has not been given its due because of its incredible complexity. It is simply astonishing, the language is stunning, the imagery innovative and probing. Somehow the poem manages to indict and celebrate the human condition at one and the same time.

To those who were aware of Merton's later interest in legends and myths, the poem would be less a surprise but by no means predictable. To those who sensed in Merton's early life an unresolved relationship with his brother, the message of the poem would not be incongruous.

The title of the poem is a mystery. "Geography," of course, would make sense. Merton's life was filled with actual or metaphoric journeys.

The "geography" of the poem is not totally dissimilar from the landscape of the *Seven Storey Mountain.* "Lograire," however, is another matter.

Sr. M. Therese Lentfoehr, a correspondent of Merton's for many years, explains the title as an adaptation of the actual name, Des Loges, of the French lyric poet Francois Villon.[54] *Loges* is a word used by foresters to describe their huts or cabins. The reference is also to the lookout post Merton once had when he was the official forester for his Trappist community. Dom James Fox intended this as a way of satisfying Merton's desire for an eremitical life during the years when official approval for a hermitage was not forthcoming.[55] "Loges" would also describe the actual hermitage, surrounded by woods, in which Merton lived while composing his epic poem.

There are further possibilities. They may work if one keeps in mind the English and Welsh ancestry of Merton and his French upbringing. "Logres" (or "Loegria") is an old name for England, found in Arthurian romances. The name derives from the Old French "Logres" or "Loengre," akin to the Welsh "Lloegr." C.S. Lewis, whom Merton read, uses the term.

The Geography of Lograire contains a prologue to the entire work, followed by four sections or cantos: South, North, East, West. The poem centers around the rise and fall of myth dreams. It focuses on the Cain-Abel myth as a means by which cultures are organized and destroyed. In the North canto, especially, Merton speaks of his personal life and journey. He integrates this into the worldview his poem envisions. The map of *The Geography of Lograire* is global human experience.

Prologue

The poem begins in the South with a dramatic opening scene. A captain, a slaver, guides his boat quietly along the waterways of the American South, searching in the dusk and darkness for a runaway black slave.

The captain is unshaven, intent, trying to catch every sound. Merton holds the scene a moment and interprets it along the lines of a cluster of myths and legends.

There is murder in the air and oppression. The memory of Cain and Abel is evoked as the mythical fratricide is reenacted in Virginia. The prologue is crowded with images of water journeys. The captain of the slave boat straining to hear a slave escaping in the woods becomes Odysseus straining to hear the siren song on the open seas leading to Ithaca.

The scene fades into Wales, the country where Owen Merton's family lived. A "child of Wales," Thomas Merton remembers a toy he once named "Tristram." Tristram, in folklore, was a wanderer. The idea of homelessness and wandering recurs on multiple levels. There is a cry in the night as a "wall wails wide" in Wales. Wales evokes images of the lost "father," of the "maps" one takes on a journey, of the "grand opposites in my blood," of home and "father-mother land." Merton was influenced by William Faulkner and his use of the South as a means of understanding the human condition. In the background of the prologue one senses the lost father of Faulkner's *Absalom, Absalom!*, the racial fratricide of *Light in August,* the family torn asunder by death and despair in *The Sound and the Fury.*

Merton evokes images of the New Testament as the hunt for the slave ensues. The river in Virginia is crimson with the blood of Abel. The blood makes the river run so that the white captain can pursue the black slave. The blood of Abel is the Blood of the Lamb, the Blood of Christ, the blood of "Jim Son Crow." The prologue is linked by images of water and by images of blood. Merton refers to the opposites in his blood, to the Celtic blood that flows in his veins, to the blood of Abel, of Christ, of blacks, of the "slain son" who represents all three, of the "slain brother" who calls down the ire of God, the "Ira Dei," the judgment against the human race whose members failed their Creator by destroying one another. The prologue closes with images of the Hebrew Bible: the snake; Abraham, who becomes a mythical symbol of fatherhood; Isaac, whose father almost lost him; the blood of the ram becoming the Blood of the Lamb.

The prologue evokes Genesis. It deals with beginnings, the beginnings of the poet's life and the origins of fratricide. It reminds us also of an end time, of judgment, of the Redeemer who will end all wars. The theme of the poem is set. This will be an epic about universal relationships and human dreams, of myth systems and homelessness.

South

The South canto consists of eleven poems. Three southern cultures are explored: the American South; the southern nations of Africa; and Mexico.

The first poem in the South canto is filled with Eucharistic symbolism. The blood is not only the blood of Abel and the Blood of the Lamb but the Blood of the Eucharistic ritual: the rosy cross; the buttercup rose; the rosy pies. The first poem ends with images of Passover and Ash Wednesday. In this new Exodus, blacks run to the red river for salvation the way the Israelites once sought safety in the Red Sea.

The Lamb seeks to save not only Abel but also Cain. Easter is a festivity not only for the Abel who is innocent but for all sinners. Even Cain must become "Paschal Cain," the "friend" of the Lamb. Cain is saved by the brother he slays. The tragedy endlessly repeated becomes the grace perpetually renewed. We are restored by those we exploit. Merton's love for dialectic is seldom more effective than in this epic. Cain and Daisy "lock their golden eyes." Daisy is a symbol for Christ, the sun/Son. The word *daisy* is derived from the Old English for "day's eye," that is, the sun. The Lamb saves the one who slaughters it.

The American South poems (poems I–IV) occur, for the most part, in Kentucky, that state in which Merton lives. The Cain-Abel saga is reenacted around "Fort Thomas," that is, in the region of Merton's hermitage. Close by is Fort Knox, where the Cain-Abel conflict continues, not as a racial contest but as a military venture. The South is portrayed as gravitating toward slave camps and military bases.

In the third poem of the South canto, Merton satirizes the false Christianity of the South, a Christianity that justified slavery with hymns and biblical texts. The poem is filled with lyrics from "Nearer, My God, to Thee," "Rock of Ages," "Swing Low, Sweet Chariot," and "Down by the Old Mill Stream." Piety and sentiment camouflage savagery and slavery. But such "religion" makes no one free.

"Miami You Are about to be Surprised," Merton sings in the fourth song of the South canto. Merton evokes images of a glittering southern city as he describes the South at play in the spray of the ocean, limbo dancing, beautiful people, suburban afternoons, Hilton candlelight.

Beneath the glittering splendor, however, there is decay. The mouths of people are filled with seaweed, their arms with holes. Messages are scrambled. Merton warns that those who read the meaning of Miami may have heart failure in their fun. Miami is about to be surprised because it is about to die.

Miami will be even more surprised to encounter a new life from its tragic death. "Miami" is a name that evokes the South and racism, but it also resonates with the memory of Native Americans who give the city its name and the Spanish conquistadores who bring to it a belligerent Christianity. Miami, furthermore, suggests the French word for "friend." New life will come to Miami, but not from the glitter and affluence. It will come when Miami is remade by sacrificial love and universal friendship. The poem ends with the theme of salvation and returns us to poem one in the American South canto. That poem began with a question about salvation: "Will a narrow lane / Save Cain?" The question is answered affirmatively at the end.

The American South poems take us from Virginia in the prologue to Kentucky and finally to Florida. The movement of the cycle of poems is farther and farther south geographically. These poems prepare the way for another series of southern poems. The Cain-Abel myth is reenacted in the United States in the black-white tension. It is necessary now to trace black roots back to Africa. Poems V–VII in the South canto move in that direction.

Africa

In Africa, the need for relationship arises again as a central theme. White missionaries have brought Christianity to the continent, but they have also instilled notions of white superiority. African culture is dismissed as aesthetically and religiously inferior. South V is a song of the Bantu tribe, a Thonga lament, in which native Africans plead for equality. They chant of the need to eat together in peace, to allow no disagreement between white and black. The poem ends with a Hottentot message that shows a deep yearning for redemption and resurrection.

In the African poems, Merton is sensitive to the native religious values of the Africans. His respect for Asian religions led him to regard favorably the instinctive religious sensibilities of the human race. His outrage at the Roman suppression of missionary efforts to accommodate Confucianism with Catholicism made him all the more determined to look carefully at the values of a culture before seeking to change them.[56]

The Western obsession with control is counterproductive to the very religious efforts of the missionaries. In South VI, entitled "How to Handle Mystics," his poem is based on a historical account in W.C. Willoughby's *Soul of the Bantu.* Missionaries in the poem become uncomfortable with the all-night prayer services and ecstatic experiences of the natives. They handle the "problem" by dispensing drugs to tranquilize the natives, convinced that religious activities must fit predetermined categories. The myths of reason, science, and medicine are more decisive than the native enthusiasm for religious experience, the very experience missionaries allegedly come to support. Mysticism makes the missionaries uneasy; they are more comfortable with institutional identity or control.

The last poem in the African cycle is entitled "Notes for a New Liturgy." In the new liturgy the white man rules the congregation. He is opposed to the witch doctor and offers what he believes to be more impressive credentials: a college degree, a title from the religious community that sponsors him, episcopal connections. The credentials are extrinsic to the inherent talent of the white ruler. This contrasts with the witch doctor, whose value must be judged in terms of his personal charism and of his community's acceptance of him.

In the new liturgy the white religious ruler chants in imperatives. "My word is final." He is a technological shaman who carries lie detectors, wristwatches, prescription drugs, Pepsi-Cola. The native liturgy of the Africans is discarded as frivolous and fanciful, superstitious and arbitrary. In its place the missionary substitutes the worship of machines, of control and efficiency, of management techniques and psychological manipulation. The new liturgy is bound up with an alien culture, a leader who exalts himself above the masses, a priest who prefers admiration from his congregation rather than service or ministry to them, a "spirituality" that violates the canons of relationship for the sake of canon law, a Church that has its own interests at heart rather than the needs of those it claims to serve.

The poems of the American South examined the violation of universal relationship by a culture riddled with racism. The poems of Africa describe a rejection of equality by a Church driven by dominion. The final poems in the South canto, poems VIII–XI, deal with slaughter and deception in Mexico.

Mexico

In South VIII, Merton describes the flower festivals and fasts of the Mayan Indians. Bishop Diego de Landa (1524–1579) studies the gentle rituals of flowers, clay, corn, dancing, bread, and music. He finds them distasteful and burns the sacred books of the Mayan people. Because of this, we know nothing of this highly developed culture except what is reported by those who had no appreciation for it and who were instruments of its destruction.

In poem nine, "The Ladies of Tlatilco," the art of Mexico and Central America is correlated with advertisements from *The New Yorker.* The former manifests a greater purity, although the latter supposedly represents progress. The ladies of Tlatilco wore nothing but turbans, and this was judged immodest. But American advertisements, allegedly modest, seduce the reader to use powders and scents described as wicked and provocative, intended to inflame eroticism. American magazines trumpet bleached hair, bubble bath, dyes and sprays. Women are encouraged to be sensuous, to dress in a fashion that tempts and teases indiscriminately. Indeed, Christian culture has elevated the status of women! Merton is satirical and humorous. He enjoys the fun of laughing at the solemnity of advertisements and the outrageous promises they make. There is also sadness in the poem because it describes a culture Christians destroyed. Only stones impervious to destruction remain. Everything gentle and fragile was torn asunder. We shall never know, Merton laments, whether they carved wood or not.

The final poems in the South canto trace the rise and fall of Mayan culture, the loss of its calendars and liturgies, the desecration of its myths and belief system. The poetry in these closing poems is both poignant and angry. It describes the mourning and "brimming tears," the burned books and the burned men, the flaming harvests and the lost traditions. The Mayans pray as they are exiled and die that their children may one day read the remnants and learn from the ashes who their fathers were.

The destruction of the civilization is engineered by priests and patriots from Spain. They bring with them adultery and rape, fornication and bribery. They appoint book burners and commission hangmen, elevating the Mayan aristocracy by lifting their heads in death.

As the South canto ends, the tears of the Mayan people merge with the tear gas American police hurl at blacks during the civil rights riots of the 1960s. Mayan bodies burned for heresy fade into the smoke arising from crowds of black American protestors as southern sheriffs throw gas grenades. The massacre of the Mayan civilization is repeated as racist Americans attack an alien culture in their midst. Mayan aristocrats look down in death from the trees on which they were hanged; police helicopters hover above blacks pleading for freedom in the cities of America. The shouts of war as Spanish conquistadores slay the Indians are drowned out by the banshee howls of police sirens assaulting the tolerance of the human ear. Americans want control over blacks and are willing to achieve this though a savagery akin to that of the Spanish who felt a need to control the Mayans.

The South canto opened with Cain in pursuit of Abel, with Christianity justifying the oppression, with images of the Eucharist and memories of a lost brotherhood and sisterhood. The canto concludes with Spanish adventurers in pursuit of Native Americans. Catholicism provides the fuel for the fires that burn censored books and censured heretics. This is justified by piety and dogma gone wild.

The canto is sad, indeed tragic. The redemptive myth does not function effectively in Christianity because the creation myth has been ignored. The equality with which the world began is not allowed to continue. Christians have at times failed to heal because they forgot that universal relationship is the point of Genesis. In such cases, the cross became a weapon of destruction rather than a symbol of love, raised over the broken bodies of men and women in whom it might have inspired hope.

North

The North canto is the only one with its own developed prologue. It is more complex than the other cantos, and the most personal. Merton fuses the memories of his own life with that of the age. He becomes a symbol of the century in which he lives.

In the prologue, Merton speaks of a journey back in memory to the ways he walked as a young man. He searches for words to explain experiences he once sustained without a word. In the second chapter of this book we considered the deep need Merton had for words. His younger life was less verbal than his adult life. He returns to the earlier years as death draws near in an effort to make them verbal also. The final lines of the prologue declare that everything about him is present in this poem.

There are four poems in the North canto. The first of these is entitled "Queens Tunnel." It centers on the years Thomas Merton lived in New York City and its environs as a boy and as a young man. Images of death and birth cluster; in this poem, as Merton observes, life and death will be even, equal.

The death imagery fills the opening lines of the poem with visions of long factory funnels, police surveillance, Mafia mobsters, tunnels that descend into the darkness. The epic writings of Homer, Virgil, Dante, Milton, Joyce describe the underworld, the land of the dead, a region of shadows and sorrows. Merton's epic includes the classic convention of such a journey into death. He himself dies soon after composing these lines. The tunnel that gives the poem its title is an even or equal symbol of life or death. The tunnel functions as a reminder of death since it takes us under the earth into a place where there is no light. The tunnel is also a symbol of birth since it leads us out of a darkness into the light. The tunnel is a death trap and a birth canal, a tomb and a womb. At its midpoint it becomes not a descent but an ascent. At its center, death passes into birth. The first symbol of the North canto fulfills the intention of the prologue where Merton speaks of equalizing life and death.

In a parody of the *Anima Christi*, a venerable Christian prayer, Merton calls on the sights and sounds and smells of Queens to bring salvation. It is a device reminiscent of the opening of Nathaniel West's *Miss Lonelyhearts*. Merton writes:

> Most holy incense burners of Elmhurst save us
> Most Coronas screen us
> House of Hungarians feed us
> Give us our Schenley labels from day to day.[57]

There is death in the air and death is reinforced by flight and fear. The poem circles the globe as Merton rushes to Rome, London, Scandinavia, Egypt, the North Sea, Scotland, southern England, Cambridge, the Thames River. In the midst of the running, John Paul dies: "Icarus falls." With the use of this classical allusion, Merton evokes the lost father. Icarus falls from the heavens and loses his father and his life. The wings of wax that allowed Icarus to fly were fashioned by his father, Daedalus. Daedalus and Icarus suggest Stephen Dedalus, the young man in James Joyce's *Ulysses*, who searches desperately for a father and finds him in Leopold Bloom. Merton was deeply influenced by Joyce, as we have seen. The Icarus allusion serves also to describe the lost brother and to indicate the manner of his dying, falling into the North Sea from mechanical wings that no longer held him aloft.

The darkness of the poem is not only the darkness of funnels and tunnels, the darkness of Icarus and John Paul as they fall away from the sun into the dark sea, it is also the inability to understand or comprehend. Merton cannot see what must be seen although he looks at everything. The poem describes a time when even the brightly burning tiger of William Blake and the mystic visions of Blake and Merton offer no clarity. In the *Seven Storey Mountain*, Merton speaks of his father reading Blake's poems to him and of his disbelief in tigers that burned bright.

Love is the evasion of death. The poem becomes a confused search for love as the adolescent Merton makes halting efforts at connecting. He is alone under a maple tree and then, all of a sudden, speaking to a girl recently returned from Curacao. Among the women he seeks is his mother and the "grey-eyed Church" which he knows is "gonna get me." There is Connie, with whom he drinks wine, and Anna, who serves liquor illegally. Ruthie brings a friend from Vassar.

The East River becomes "winedark," as the mad race for love lurches between Coney Island and Astoria. But Coney Island is not Ithaca. The search for home must continue. The love turns to lust and violence as the search becomes desperate, frantic. There is panic in the air. A woman is raped on the streets of New York and no one answers her cries for help. People become indifferent to their common bonds with one another. Lady Chatterley and her lover, pornographic movies, make the rounds of the city. Out of the chaos there emerge slowly and gently images of purity, of love that does not turn to greed, of relationships that elude even death. There is the "Virgin Mother of lilylight," the "lost nun in the infirmary nightlight" and a poignant line in which Merton runs "for the vanished nurse in the subway tunnels of every night." Famous Tom, as he calls himself, "sleeps wailing for a mate." The wailing fuses with the wails in Wales with which *The Geography of Lograire* begins.

Toward the end of the poem, Merton weeps in lines that recall the psalms of exile: "...I sat down and wept by Sandy river..." There are images of Blake with tigers that burn in the night and memories of a bare room in Great Britain where Merton saw "my Baby" and recalls the child's mother "laid out on a long white table." The lost father is now Merton and the lost son is not only the son of Owen but the son of Thomas.

"Geography is in trouble all over Lograire," as the poem ends. Religion is in disarray, home is "underwater," memories have been put on audiotape rather than shared among the living; conscience has been silenced so that it serves autocratic systems. There is the smell of gunpowder in the night, and in the morning there are bodies among the willows. Even Christ has been made by the Church and the colonializers into a white man rather than a universal brother. When Christ goes to Harlem and comes among his own they know him not because race has assumed a greater force in the society than life or love. Indeed, life and love depend upon the race by which one is identified. Christ is now Icarus, fallen from the heavens into institutional Christianity and Western society. The ultimate sin against universal love is to have made Christ a savior of only one race so that all other cultures and religions are deprived of him.

The first poem of the North canto is a difficult piece because so many of the memories are personal and fragmentary, emerging from the subconscious and the troubled conscience of the poet. The poem shows Merton at his candid best, absorbing the shock of the century and the fury of his own personal search. The poem is filled with images of seeing, of looking and yet not having vision, of surveillance that observes human activity and misses the human dimension. Spies and police, watchmen and guards are posted, but none of them sees the pain of Merton or counts as important his prayers in the night. The onlookers are bystanders. The observers neither participate nor appreciate the suffering one sustains in order to live. The substance of life is neglected in the detailed investigations into human behavior.

Yet somehow there is light in Lograire. The light shines in a terrifying darkness that is threatened by its clarity. The tunnel is a way out of the brightness. But the tunnel is part of the problem. In Lograire one has great need of an eye doctor, need for a light, an Ahura Mazda, that will allow people to see life. The tunnel is part of the problem but fortunately it is the "Queens Tunnel" with all the imagery this suggests. Mary is Queen of Heaven, Queen of Light. It is light week in Lograire. The tunnel belongs to the Virgin as well as to the wanton woman.

Throughout the poem, Merton searches for his mother. The *Geography of Lograire* is in many ways more revealing than the *Seven Storey Mountain* and the journals because it speaks in the symbols of poetry and in the free association the subconscious allows. "Sing a song to Mamma…" he chants as he tries to answer the death letter his mother wrote him as a child. A few lines later he describes another kind of motherhood, the girl he made pregnant and the child he never really knew.

The journey through Merton's psyche takes us through fields where "light" and "wine" and Franciscan simplicity abound. All the men are called "Frank," a name Merton took as a code name when he became a Young Communist, a name associated with the religious community, the Franciscans, he first wanted to join. The poem is a search for the feminine dimension in his own life symbolized by the vanished nurse, the lost nun, the missing mother, the Queen of Heaven. Reality becomes confused as images of purity succeed images of erotic women whose breasts are displayed on posters in New York City. The poet wails for a mate and dreams often of women who might bring him life and light. The yearning is not physical so much as spiritual; the object, not always another person but the feminine side of his own nature. The need may be sexual, but it is, on a deeper level, a need to complete the unfinished relationship with his own mother.

Mother Church beckons Merton as seductively and as surely as the women who crowd this poem. Christ is the final figure in the poem, a Christ who comes to the wanderer without waiting for the frightened pilgrim to find him, a Christ who "went down to stay...and took his place with them at table." The promise of Christ is not yet fully effective because he is a Christ of the white race only. The words of the promise, however, are an answer to the confusion the poet has experienced: "It is very simple much simpler than you imagine." Early in the poem, prayer was but a parody: "Most holy incense burners of Elmhurst save us." As the poem ends, prayer is answered and Christ has come to New York.

In the second poem of the North canto, Merton is in England as a youngster and comes alive to his first sexual experiences. He is "a grain of fear" at this time in his life, a child who must "die into manhood," but also a sensitive person who finds no answers to the shameless questions his young heart asks of life.

In the third and fourth poems the theme of racial murder, the myth of Cain and Abel, is continued.

The third poem is one of religious persecution and parallels the South canto poems, which dealt with the suppression of religious experience in Africa by missionaries (South VI–VII) and in Mexico by the Spaniards (South VIII–XI). In the present poem, the scene is London and the persecutors are the English. Drawing from a book by Norman Cohn, *The Pursuit of the Millennium*, Merton describes the torture inflicted on a group called Ranters.

The Ranters were a fanatical cult that arose in England in the seventeenth century. Their unconventional behavior moved from mysticism to license. The point of the poem is not the excesses of the Ranters but the desire for those in authority to control unsanctioned activity. This control amounts to barbarism as the persecutors call for burning people's tongues. The savagery is justified by a supposed need for orthodoxy and for order. The poem quotes from tracts of the times, court trials, Acts of Parliament, pamphlets.

The Ranters are accused of comparing God to a great ocean whose measure no one can take. Such mysticism is judged intolerable because it places God beyond our control. The Ranters are criticized for seeing God everywhere and thus appearing to be pantheistic. They are indicted for believing that everyone will be saved at the end of time and thus opening a way to unbridled optimism and to a salvation that is uncontrollable. Ranters are charged with excessive attention to the promptings of the Spirit, leading to licentious and violent actions. The complaints against the Ranters reflect an uneasiness with mysticism rather than a concern with admitted excesses. The sexual license of which the Ranters are accused is judged more obscene than the mutilation and burning of their bodies by the "devout."

White Wilderness

Merton had a sense of drama about the sea. His description of the riverboat captain hunting slaves at the beginning of *The Geography of Lograire* is visually powerful. He again conjures up captivating imagery in poem four, the closing poem of the North canto. Entitled "Kane Relief Expedition," the poem is based on James Laws's *Journal of the Kane Relief Expedition 1855.*

The voyage is a desperate search in the waters west of Greenland and east of Baffin Island for a lost group of Arctic explorers, the Kane expedition. In the previous water voyage of the South canto, the riverboat captain sailed through the pine and mist of sweet-smelling Virginia.

Now the seascape is stark; the storms are savage. The region is described as an Eden, but Eden is not adazzle with color. It is silver-severe. The horizon is empty.

There is an ominous silence throughout this final poem. This is not a southern landscape where thrushes fill the air with song, or a northern city where life screeches to signal its presence. We are in a country where icebergs are church-quiet on a Sunday morning and slow-sail past the ship. The scene is surrealistic, somewhat reminiscent of Edgar Allen Poe's tale of terror on the ice in *The Narrative of A. Gordon Pym.* Icebergs take on the shapes of women dressed in white as if a magician had converted them into praying figures. It is difficult to know if the figures are human or inanimate, or whether they pray to save the ship or sink it.

Icebergs collapse on one another as the ship heads north. Whales accompany the ship, but whether they are curious or malevolent is not clear. The poem depicts a land and a season where friend and enemy are not easily distinguished.

Out of the blinding whiteness, a boat with six Eskimos, followed by innumerable kayaks, approaches the ship and pleads with the whites to buy the fish they sell. The ship is near land. The expedition anchors and visits a settlement consisting of twelve cabins. High on the wet and slippery rocks above the encampment the sailors visit a graveyard where bodies are buried under stones and in crevices waiting for life through an endless winter. The crew of the ship dance with the native girls, alive and warm, in contrast to the dead they had visited and the frost that engulfs them.

The ship moves on through Devil's Thumb, the grave of twenty-eight whaling vessels sunk in but one year, and finds Melville Bay with all the emotions the name evokes of Herman Melville and the doomed search for Moby Dick.

The ship lands again. A circle of tents greets it. The Indian inhabitants hoot like owls, the symbol of death. The tent dwellers communicate with the whites in sign language, intensifying the eerie silence. The signals indicate that the Kane party was crushed on the ice. This point is made clear when a clay pipe is smashed in the hands of the narrator. The natives wear knives that resemble the ivory-handled weapons the Kane party once carried. The ice and the sailors and the ivory knives are white. White seems to be the color of death. The white moon appears in the heavens and the setting becomes a fairy scene of mountains bursting with light of a strange luminescence in the awful darkness of the Arctic night.

At midnight, September 4, 1855, a gale engulfs the rescue ship, smashing it against a white mass four times its size, hurling it headlong into horror. The ship is splintered into its component parts and sinks, torn asunder by the hurricane that pulls it upward and the waves that reach up to draw it down.

The North canto ends with the howling wilderness of the white sea. The white race is defeated in its effort to turn Eskimo culture and frozen resources into capital and dominion. Ships and weapons are brought into the circle of the Arctic; native women are exploited for pleasure; native men, for profit. The white man is Cain, hunter of the Eskimo in the North, of the blacks in the South. The whites die in the North, not at the hands of their brothers, but by the geographical extension of their lust and greed. The Eskimo does not kill the whites. Neither did the blacks.

The whites are defeated by their rush into a region they cannot tame. The ice is as frozen as the cold reasoning power of the northern Anglo-Saxon race. The native races die by murder, but whites die by their suicidal refusal to respect limits, by their anxiety to extend control beyond the bounds of the very reason they cherish as their greatest resource. The white icebergs, like the white race, are symbols of rigidity, massive power, haughty pretension. The glaciers, like the white race, are symbols of a superiority that allows no equality. The white myth dream, Merton observes elsewhere, focuses on absolute superiority, total dominion.

The North canto begins in America and focuses on the nightmare side of New York City. The canto is tense and nervous. Frenzy is in the air; anxiety bristles in the atmosphere. The violence here is different from that of the South canto, where savagery is localized. There it is directed against particular groups for specific reasons. In the North, however, the violence is aimless, unfocused. In the "Queens Tunnel" poem, New York City turns on itself in self-destruction. In poems two and three, sex predominates. But the sex is purposeless. The adolescent Merton and the licentious Ranters use sex for its own sake. In poem four, the nightmare comes full circle. Whites dance with native girls beneath a mountain graveyard. Storms are created in the Arctic darkness. Nature avenges the hubris and arrogance, the coldness and insolence, the greed and the lust.

The canto opened with thoughts of death and the Queens Tunnel that led to the land of the dead. The canto ends with death and the glaciers that inflict it. The tall funnels of the city at the beginning of the North canto and the huge icebergs at the end form a skyscape of horror. The smoke of the chimneys in New York City and the hurricanes of the Arctic become symbols of fatality. Mortality mocks human ambition and limits human power.

East

The North and South cantos center on racial antagonism. The East and West cantos focus on cultural conflicts. In these latter poems, people are violent with one another not because of skin color but because of different traditions and values. There is some overlap. Race and culture frequently intermingle and form an excuse for hostility. For the most part, however, cultural disparity is the source of homicidal contention in these final cantos. The Cain-Abel myth is again operative, but in another key.

There are ten poems in the East canto. Cargo cults and cargo songs act as a thread unifying the canto. The South canto ended with hummingbirds in the air and ropes for lynching. There were sentences in Spanish and sentences of death. The sounds of Romance languages and the screams of murder merged with the whirring of police helicopters and the combustion of tear gas grenades as the hunt for the "inferior" race was pursued. The North canto ended with the howling of the wind, the crashing of ice, the cracking of a wooden ship, the desperate cries for help that could not be heard above the roar and the rage of the sea. The East canto will end with plaintive songs in the night, cargo songs praying for a better world, a new life, another choice.

The first poem in the East canto is based on a travel record written by a fourteenth-century Muslim writer, Ibn Battuta. The record is entitled *Travels in Asia and Africa 1325–1356*. Merton worked with a translation from the Arabic by H.A.R. Gibb.

The East canto opens with a shocking scene that precedes the first poem in the series. It is an eleven-line prelude to the East. A slave proves his love for his sultan by cutting off his own head after having made a long speech describing that love. A Westerner, observing the decapitation, finds the custom quaint. The short passage keynotes the entire canto. The East is inscrutable to Western intelligence. The West views the custom as quaint. There is a touch of arrogance in the description, an arrogance that allows one to dismiss that which is unintelligible.

Westerners observe the East with clinical detachment. They analyze human behavior in the East in much the same way as they might comment on animal laboratory experiments or scientific studies of inorganic phenomena. It is not brother who meets brother, for example, in the encounter of West and East but a rationalist, intrigued and curious with cultural behavior judged as somehow subhuman. The slave who decapitates himself may not exhibit praiseworthy behavior, but the point is not the slave's action but the Western observer who dismisses without seeking to understand.

The East canto opens with the chanting of the Koran. It closes with the songs of the cargo cult. The canto moves from the sophisticated cultural achievement of the Arabic world to the diverse cultures of New Guinea.

Thomas Merton demonstrates a more refined critical approach to the East in this poem than in his early prose writing. The first poem in the canto contains seven sections. Its format is that of a travelogue, narrated by Ibn Battuta. Merton does not exalt the East as an apparently problem-free area of the world but shows its shortcomings in the first poem.

The East is troubled by ethnic and religious persecution, by arbitrary slaughter, warfare, and the compulsions of an orthodoxy so unsure of itself that it tortures and murders dissenters. To this extent, the East offers no helpful alternatives to the West.

The visual and sensuous imagery of the first poem is unforgettable. It describes life in Cairo, Mecca, Isfahan, Delhi, Calicut. In Cairo, Merton writes of mystics and sugar, of cantors and soap, of prophets and oil. The culture is religiously and economically rich. Merton describes a group of heretics who are slaughtered with swords and dismembered. The dead number twenty thousand. The murdered heretics are reminiscent of the persecuted Ranters in the North canto and the decimated

Mayans in the South canto. Orthodoxy leads to homicide. The broken bodies of slain brethren East, North, and South are eloquent witness against rigid orthodoxy.

The description of the opulence of the East continues beyond Cairo to the other sections of the first poem. In Mecca, prayer and perfume are described; in Isfahan and Delhi we read of orchards and banquets, of apricots and pears, of melons and exotic cooking over candlelight, of people who sit in midair and of religion used as entertainment and magic. In Calicut, we are made to experience the Malabar coast and gingery pepper spice, palm leaf baskets and sandalwood.

The poem is beautiful, but underneath the luxury and enchantment there is decay. The contrast of glitter and decay is reminiscent of the Miami poem in the South canto. The chants from the Koran do not overcome the cries of fear and pain as people are murdered or the shouts of rage and hatred as men are hunted. The Fall has come to the East. Its fruit, however, is not the rich, sweet food that hangs from the trees in the eternal spring of Arabia but the bitterness that drives Cain to shed the blood of Abel.

In the second poem, "East with Malinowski," Merton elaborates on a journal from the South Sea Islands written by Bronislaw Malinowski in the second decade of the twentieth century. Malinowksi is physically ill, sexually obsessed, socially offensive during his visit to observe the natives. He speaks in detail of his vomiting, of urination from the cliffs, and defecation in the water. He befouls the environment and the culture. The bronze bodies of men are targets for his guns; the breasts of women are objects of his erotic desire. In the polite atmosphere at a hotel in Port Moresby, New Guinea, Malinowski shares sherry and gramophone music with his fellow whites and tells him how vulgar the native women are. The contrast is graphic and tragic. A man violates a culture, exploits its innocence, pollutes its terrain, and then criticizes its vulgarity. The colonizer shows neither compassion nor decency, neither conscience nor restraint.

Cargo Songs

The third poem in the East canto begins the cargo songs. The cults of Melanesia and New Guinea will figure throughout the remainder of this canto. Merton based his material for this section on a series of anthropological studies.

The cargo cults were discussed earlier in this chapter. The cults originate near the end of the nineteenth century and flourish after World War II. They are a means of handling cultural change by rituals designed to enchant the deities. We have seen how this behavior is also present in the West but in a camouflaged form. The cults are messianic and salvific. They seek safety in commerce and power, magic and mime. In Melanesia and New Guinea, the magic is incantatory and the mime is identified with the imitation of white merchants and technicians. In the West, the magic is the illusion one conveys to others, the appearances and public relations approaches that make others think we are more powerful than we are in actual fact. The mimicry is the imitation of the majority or the powerful, the famous or the elite, the successful or the wealthy.

The first cargo song begins with an account of an English governor, Sir William MacGregor, who is compulsive about sitting higher than any other native in his presence. He tears a native chief by the hair from a platform he occupies when the native is more elevated than the white master. The poem ends with Bronislaw Malinowski shouting that the brutes should be exterminated. He is angered because the natives stole the tobacco he offered to have them stand still until he took a photograph. Such insolence must be met by death. The white man brings death in this poem, sometimes killing from anger, sometimes killing as lesson. Few things seem to impress the natives more than public, systematic executions.

In this cargo song, the natives react. They run to the hills, in a scene reminiscent of the flight of Tucker Caliban, and discard the artifacts of European civilization; tobacco and rifles, matches and tools. They forsake Christianity also with its holy water and celibacy, its indulgences and indults, its obsession with sex and authority. Malinowski cries for the extermination of the brutes. The natives hear in his demands the voice of the European West and the sound of institutional Christianity. They want no part of either. It is difficult, however, to struggle free, as poems four and five make clear. The technology the West exports is seductive. It fascinates as well as subjugates. The process of colonization has entered the souls of the natives, so that rebellion against the West can never be total.

Poems VI–X show how deeply the psyche of South Sea natives has been influenced. These poems deal with the cargo cults in detail.

In poem six, the natives build a warehouse in the hope that God will fill it with meat, soup, razor blades, flashlights, and hydrogen peroxide. They ritually wash away their impurities, visit their dead, and pray that their heavenly Father will send them help since they have no Jeeps, ships, or planes, not even hammers to work with or pants to wear. The cult is organized around Kaum, a prophet and liturgist for the group. Kaum was a historical figure imprisoned by the Australians in 1944 for inciting rebellion. The white rulers are alarmed when they learn of the warehouse and demand it be torn down, its timbers carried eighteen miles to the sea and there discarded.

Poem seven is an effort to render in pidgin English a New Guinea equivalent of Genesis. The Fall is described in terms of whiskey and sex. Adam and Eve are punished when God does not allow them a can opener for the canned food of Eden. Later, Noah builds a steamer and takes on board cargo as well as animals. Noah stocks the steamer with instant coffee, tobacco, candy bars, and matches. The steamer lands in Australia after the Flood. One of Noah's sons, Ham, is exiled to New Guinea because he laughs at Noah's intoxication and nakedness. Ham is black and is forbidden cargo. The other sons of Noah are white and grow up in Sydney, Australia, with cargo.

The natives complain that the Bibles they are given by missionaries have been censored. The pages on how to get cargo are missing. The natives are convinced, however, that their ancestors are busy in the sky above Sydney putting meat into cans and affixing labels that will ensure that they get to the natives without being lost en route. Natives are lacking in cargo because whites change the labels written by their ancestors on the ships from Australia and address them instead to white missionaries, government officials, planters, police. The implication in the native version of economic inequality is that all have a right to an equal share in the world's goods. The problem facing the natives is how to get cargo directly from heaven without using the ships and planes the whites own. Fusing their native insights with Christianity, they reason that Jesus might do this for them.

The seventh poem is entitled "Cargo Catechism." We are instructed not only about the beginnings of creation and the Fall but also about "Jesus with the Cargo." Jesus is ready to save the natives, and so they gather flowers for his coming. The whites are disturbed by the frantic flower gathering, judge it as part of an organized resistance, and arrest those who make bouquets. Flower arrangement is viewed as a subversive activity. Merton's description of the flower rebellion is built on the historical figure of Ya Li, a charismatic cult leader. In actual fact, security police were busy destroying flowers and searching homes of natives for hidden, seditious bouquets. Meanwhile, Jesus is believed to be in a hotel room in Sydney with cargo but cannot leave because the whites will not bring him a suit. One day he will come and the natives will shower him with their concealed bouquets.

In the next poem, "John the Volcano," Merton attempts to work on two levels simultaneously. He continues to be interested in the phenomenon of the cargo cult and of the needs it symbolized. But he is also fascinated by the white colonists and their reaction to behavior they cannot comprehend. He places two myth systems in tension with each other.

In this poem there are riots and rumors of riots. The riots are surprisingly nonviolent. On one occasion the natives run into a store, leap over the counters, and tear price tags from the merchandise. They apparently believe there is magic in the labels that will help them obtain the merchandise. The police move swiftly and solemnly, calling the incident the "affair of the tickets," punishing natives who do not respect the pieces of paper attached to the white race's possessions. This convinces the natives that there is indeed a great significance in the price tags.

On another occasion natives bury coconuts in tremendous numbers and with an intensity the police judge alarming. The police see a plot in the planting. They are kept busy for days demanding the natives dig up the coconuts. The whites feel safe when the natives obey and the dangerous coconuts are unearthed.

The colonizers become weary from constant surveillance. But they are satisfied that their search-and-destroy missions have seized flowers, price labels, and coconuts.

The whites are obsessed with the cults because they see them as seditious. The natives, however, are seeking only for a way to define themselves with dignity. They take nothing of value from the colonists and yet they seem to be taking everything. Whites feel deprived by this activity because there is no place of equality for the native in the white myth system. Although natives have been exploited and subjugated, whites continue to view them suspiciously. Especially troubling is the lack of gratitude on the part of the natives. Paternalistic systems, civil or ecclesiastical, regularly deem dependents insensitive and ungrateful.

In actual fact, whites are filled with hostility and fear. Paternalism masks a disdain toward those it keeps in check. Paternalism is a system superficially benign but essentially acquisitive. Granted the proper conditions, paternalism moves from superficial courtesy to savage suppression.

The natives chant their songs, organize moonlit processions, hurl money into the sea (perhaps to buy a ship of cargo), dream of radios and prefabricated houses, play guitars, sound bells, and hope that God will answer and send cargo. The whites are mystified even though the cult of cargo and commerce, the belief that dignity has something to do with possessions, is a white myth. The natives actually wish no harm to the whites, merely, a recognition of their humanity. They cry out for meaning but the whites read the cry as rebellion, insurrection, a disorder. History has shown, as the white myth interprets it, that one race is superior and that some races cannot manage their own affairs or address their own religious instincts. Natives dishonor nature and God when they suppose that their traditions and religious doctrines are equal to European or Christian interpretations of the world.

The final poems of the East canto are songs of death and resurrection. The ninth poem relates a violent incident in the cargo cult when a white man is slain and cannibalized. The nonviolence has turned to violence, at least in this isolated incident. The cannibalism is a last desperate effort by the natives to become white or, at least, to learn the secret and the magic of the white control of cargo. The poem is a brutal description of death, of the death of a white man but also of the death of hope in the natives for a life of human recognition. The poem has a number of references to resurrection. The natives wish to live again, the way the whites do now, in a land of no more death.

The tenth and concluding poem in the canto ends with a prayer by the natives that the white race and the natives become one family. The prayer begins with a plea for tobacco and cigarette paper, but it moves to the real point of the petition. It is a yearning for happiness and for skin that is white if this be the only way to happiness in this world. The prayer is a cry of people whose hope in themselves and in their own culture has been destroyed. It is the expression of a people bewildered by change, alienated from their traditions and rituals.

The canto opened in violence as a slave cut off his head to please his sultan. It ends in a despair even more terrible as an entire race commits psychological suicide. The slave died believing his death demonstrated his love for the sultan. The emotional death of the natives is worse. It is motivated not by love but by anguish. Their death has no meaning unless they can return as whites, who apparently have inherited the earth and enchanted God. The slave belonged to the sultan in life and in death. The natives never belonged anywhere, to anyone.

West

There are four poems in the West canto. The canto begins at O'Hare Airport in Chicago and ends with Native American Ghost Dancers on the plains of the West. In the West, where the sun sets, the epic will end.

The South canto began with river travel; the North, with tunnel and automobile travel; the East, with travel by foot and the account of a fourteenth-century pilgrim; the West canto opens with airplanes and passengers waiting at a mammoth airport.

The first poem is entitled, "Day Six O'Hare Telephane." Each word is significant. The sixth day of creation is the day human beings receive life in the Genesis account. O'Hare is, of course, the name of the airport. "Telephane" is an amalgam of telephone and cellophane, a symbol of artificiality in human communication. The sixth day of creation is the beginning and the end. The Fall occurs, and in the Fall reality is clouded by illusion.

The poem is concerned with illusion. Viewed from the plane, the world is a lake of cotton, a milky mist. A Buddhist passenger speaks occasionally, reminding his audience that all is illusion. His sentences are quotations from an obscure Vedantic book Merton was reading.[58] The plane trip has as its destination Mount Rushmore. In a world of illusion, people trust in the solidity of Mount Rushmore and in the stone images of the American presidents enshrined there.

Reality, however, is more pliable. There is no permanence in life any more than there is real movement toward human development in airplanes or real communication by telephone or real progress in cellophane. Things made by machine (airplanes, telephones, cellophane) do not, in themselves, put people in touch with one another or improve human wisdom. Communication problems begin on day six of creation with failure in dialogue and human understanding between Adam and Eve, humans and God, Cain and Abel.

We fail because we think we are different from one another. The anonymous Buddhist reminds us that we are Brahman or God, and all is one. Machines mask the unity. This unity is the one reality, which the West believes to be an illusion. It prefers the illusion that all are different. From the plane, the earth below manifests itself as harmonious. A change in the angle of vision shows us a harmonious world if we are willing to see it and understand it on a deeper level.

If we grasp our oneness, all the religious symbols converge. The one earth, which one sees so clearly from the plane, gives us, in the examples used by Merton, Christ-Wheat, Buddha-Rice, Square Maize, and Shiva-Cake. The Christian, Buddhist, Native American, and Hindu truth represented by these symbols is one truth. The symbols also converge in their use of nourishment as the operative matrix for the symbol. We all participate in life by what we eat: wheat and rice, corn and bread. West (Christian) and East (Buddhist) are one; Native American (West) and Hindu (East) are connected. We travel together in the same plane, over the same earth, toward a common destination.

Day six of creation was not only the day on which the Fall begins but the last day on which we are all alone. Day six becomes in the poem not only the memory of a lost unity but a hope for future reunification. If the Buddhist travels in the Western plane and the Western passengers hear a monk speak about the Hindu sacred books, universal harmony may be possible. Western science (represented by the plane, by O'Hare, by the telephone, by cellophane) and Asian wisdom (symbolized by Buddhist monasticism and Hindu philosophy) can make the world and the human race whole once again. Myth systems are not complete until they nourish one another.

The second poem in the West canto concerns itself with the symbols of the American myth dream. Politicians campaign for Congress; Washington's cherry tree is celebrated; there are allusions to bumper crops, national archives, the FBI, Shirley Temple, the Roosevelts, automobiles, and nuclear arsenals.

The final two poems in the canto and in the epic deal with the Ghost Dance. The Ghost Dance originated in 1869 among the Paviotso (Paiute) Indians near Walker Lake, Nevada. The dance, actually a religious movement, spread throughout the Native American nations in the western section of the United States. The Ghost Dance was a messianic and apocalyptic ritual. The dances invited the end of history, pleaded for the return of the dead, hoped for the restoration of lands. They were an ordeal born of frenzy, an experience of ecstasy and fatigue, a movement to coax life out of the decay of indigenous civilization. They were a sign of desperation developed by those who could no longer hope in the present.

Poem three, "Ghost Dance: Prologue," is based on events which occurred in 1890, east of the Rocky Mountains; poem four, "Ghost Dance," describes a phase of the movement which originated in 1870, west of the Rockies. Chronologically, the order of the poems should be reversed; thematically, however, the present sequence makes sense.

In a book written near the end of his life, *Ishi Means Man*, Merton had occasion to deal with the Ghost Dance in detail. The Ghost Dance emerged from the spiritual loss of two civilizations in conflict. White America forced Native Americans into a situation where extreme alternatives seemed necessary. Native American nations were cut off from their cosmos. The land on which they originated is not only a source of livelihood but the basis of religion and mythology. The land is viewed as a universal right, subject to no ownership, in much the same way as white Americans consider air an element belonging to everyone. In the myth system of white Americans, land was also crucial as a means to identity but the identity was built on power and money rather than religion and tradition. In the clash of the two cultures, the Cain-Abel conflict is renewed.

The Ghost Dances, like the Cargo Cults, are fueled by the same energy and hope that lay behind the doctrine of Christian eschatology. There will be a time of universal retribution, of community and justice that cannot be undermined. There will be one family at the end of history when no further evil will be possible and no breaking of the bonds allowed.

In poem one of the West canto, Merton equates the Mayan Square Maize with the Christ-Wheat, Buddha-Rice, Shiva-Cake ritual of other religions. The Mayans created a Cruzob, or "Speaking Cross," ritual, motivated by the same objectives as the Ghost Dance ceremony. Cultists knew that a native ventriloquist projected his words from behind the cross, but they obeyed them as though God had spoken. The rite was another demonstration of the need an enslaved people experienced for a recognition of their dignity.

The Mayans created their own God from the Christian myth, a God who did not favor only the whites, a God who regarded them the way Christians seldom did. The Cruzob, or "Speaking Cross," phenomenon included a Eucharistic ritual with corn and honey in place of bread and wine. When Merton refers to the rite in poem one, it is during the passage of the jet airplane over Native American lands on the way from Chicago to Mount Rushmore. Mount Rushmore represents an American myth of ancestors seen as presidents. The Cruzob is also a search for ancestors, tradition, and roots. The Mayans who followed this rite called themselves "People of the Cross." In Latin America, they were often exterminated under the sign of the cross. In Mayan ritual, they were restored by it.

The third poem in the West canto sings a sad song of broken promises and bad faith. Native Americans complain of lands confiscated, of food denied, of pressure to conform to the norms of white society. The Indian nations were flattered with respect until they signed treaties they did not always understand. Then there was no more dialogue, no more dignity.

The poem is based on a statement made by American Horse in council and forwarded to the U.S. Indian Office, November 27, 1890. Merton read the document in James Mooney's *The Ghost-Dance Religion and the Sioux Outbreak of 1890.* American Horse was a leader on the Sioux reservations in the Dakotas. The jet plane in poem one has as its destination the Dakotas in general and Mount Rushmore in particular, as we know. The statement by American Horse complains of broken promises by the American president in Washington. The plane ride to Mount Rushmore has as its object a visit to the national shrine of the American presidency.

In poem four the Ghost Dance is dealt with more fully. A messianic figure, Wudziwob (Wovoka), preaches at Pyramid Lake in the wilderness that the dead are coming back with the Supreme Ruler to end all distinctions between the races. The sermon is poignant. Mothers will return to their children; fathers, to their sons. The ancestors must find their people dancing, happy. The dancing must continue through the night, around the fires, sometimes led by figures whose bodies glow with the phosphorus rubbed on them. In the morning, all must wash in the river.

Other dances occur, not at Pyramid Lake, but at Lost River. These dances are done in the winter with no grass growing on the earth. In the morning the washing in the river is painful; the dancers have ice in their hair.

The Cornwallis (Oregon) *Gazette* of January 4, 1873, describes the dances and the paint and the feathers. The newspaper account tells of promises at the dance that one day the Indians shall be given again their hunting grounds and peaceful homes. The whites become alarmed and believe their fear more than the report of the Superintendent of the Reservation that the dances will not lead to attacks on the whites. Merton uses as his source for this poem "The 1870 Ghost Dance" by Cora Du Bois.

The West canto ends with the death of all hope for the Native American nations. The Ghost Dance becomes a curiosity rather than a source of fear when the genocide of Native Americans is far advanced. The nations are so weakened that they will never emerge as a counter-force to white dominion. Whites now urge the remaining Indians to dance the quaint and curious Ghost Dance. The dance offers as little threat as the slave in the East canto who severs his head before his sultan. That action was also described as quaint.

The dance is now theater rather than liturgy. All the elements are there: the love of ancestors, the yearning for a lost tradition, the hope for one human family, the need for fathers and mothers to return, the joy for the land, and the lingering trust that promises might be honored. The symbol system of the dance remains. But the faith is lost. The dance is a parody of hope, a dance of despair, a dance of death. The Ghost Dance once trusted in universal love and awaited the end of history and a kingdom of justice. It now signals the demise of Native Americans in the blood of Abel shed on the plains of America.[59]

Conclusion

The Geography of Lograire is the most difficult and one of the most important of Thomas Merton's books. It shows him on the eve of his death ready to enter into a comprehensive stage of his development. His vision is now global; his instincts for universality refined, and dynamic.

The epic also manifests a talent for the dramatic. The images he evokes are haunting: the unshaven slave captain; the hunted black man; flower festivals and burned books in Mexico; the Queens Tunnel in Manhattan and the glaciers that sink a ship in the Arctic; the slave who decapitates himself in strange affection; the hope for a messiah in the East; the opulence of Asian food and festival; the cargo cults of Melanesia and the jet planes roaring across the United States; Congress and cherry trees and nuclear bombs; and finally, the Ghost Dances on the plains of the West. The learning of Merton is breathtaking; his capacity for synthesis ingenious and enlightening.

We read in *The Geography of Lograire* the history of a human family tragically torn asunder but pathetically persistent in its dream for harmony. From the pain of his own relationship with his brother, Merton forges an epic that traces the roots of our despair to the way we fail one another. From the loss of his own father, he has fashioned a poem in which all are children in search of a living parent. It is a poem that hopes for a home that perhaps will always be denied us, but a home we will dream of until the last dance is done.

CHAPTER SEVEN

Winter Rain

Cables carried the news that Thomas Merton was dead. They were cables to the abbey from a land as exotic as Lograire. The end was sudden: He was electrocuted; it was an accident. That morning, in Bangkok, he had given a talk about Marxism and monasticism, about the need for himself and all those in formal religious communities to see themselves as marginal people. In the afternoon, a fan, a faulty wire, and he knew death for the last time. It was the tenth of December, twenty-seven years to the day since he had rung the bell at Gethsemani and asked if they would take him home, make him their brother.

It had been a dramatic life. In death the symbolism remained rich. He died on a journey. At the end, he was still far from home. He died in the East. He died full of life, in the midst of posing further questions, searching in Asia for answers it could not give him. In the Eastern manner, the questions were answered with a further question, a deeper mystery. The koan this time was Merton's own death.

In a sense, he had exhausted life. His range of interest was cosmic and encyclopedic. He wrote of hermits and atom bombs, of Zen Buddhism and riots in Los Angeles, of poetry and ecumenical councils. His words were multiplied in two dozen languages. His words were always the best part of him. They remain.

He changed over the years. There is a boyish charm in the *Seven Storey Mountain*, a joy in faith, an incandescence. It is filled with wonder and surprise. It is fresh and vital. It is young and knows it is young. *Conjectures of a Guilty Bystander* is the less certain statement of a man who tried to relate his spirituality to the suffering of the world. In a letter written to the philosopher Jacques Maritain in 1960 he tells of his desire to understand all who suffer. The joy remains, but pain has become its companion. The incandescence is not lacking, but it shines more fitfully against a background of deeper darkness. There is an air of vitality about him, always this, but he speaks now of death. He senses autumn in the inner climate of his own body; there is a lateness in the season of his soul. A few years after he writes about his death and speaks about the autumn of life, it is December. It is near winter when he dies. It was near winter when he entered Gethsemani. He was buried in the rain, a winter rain that fell unexpectedly as his body was lowered in the earth.

Thomas Merton was a universal human being, an internationalist, and yet there is something typically American about him. In a study on Thomas Merton's life, James Thomas Baker finds in Merton a recapitulation of three stages of development in American religious thought. The seventeenth and eighteenth centuries are characterized by the Puritan stage of following God into the wilderness. This is paralleled by Merton's search for God in the forests and hills of Kentucky. Nineteenth-century American revivalism is reflected in Merton's spiritual writings from 1948–1958. The point of this work was conversion of life, renewal of faith. The twentieth-century social-gospel phase, an era when reform and redemption of society were the central focus, is matched by the last ten years of Merton's life. This was a time when civil rights, nonviolence, criticism of Vietnam, protest against encroaching technology occupied him.

There are other tendencies in American life that Merton reflected. Merton was inconsistent. In this, he was not at odds with the national temper. Inconsistency occurs more often when experience rather than reason or volition becomes the norm for behavior. By crowding multiple, sometimes contradictory, experiences into our respective lives we frequently violate laws of logic and inner coherence. Ralph Waldo Emerson once observed that "a foolish consistency is the hobgoblin of little minds." Emerson's point had something to do with the need to change as we develop. In this also, Merton was a representative American. Beneath the change, however, there was a striking continuity. The psychic roots of his life kept him searching for the same fundamental answers. His interests in Asia, social reform, and personal integrity were early as well as late.

There was also a touch of Henry David Thoreau in him. The abbey was his Walden; the hermitage, his cabin; Cistercian spirituality, the simple life; monasticism, his counterculture protest; conscience, his act of civil disobedience and ecclesiastical noncompliance. Emerson and Thoreau were individualists and therefore at times inconsistent. Merton, likewise, was critical and creative and would not continue doggedly in one direction very long.

Emerson and Thoreau reflect the American tradition of asceticism and contemplation. The tradition began with the Puritans and continues in the various utopian American experiments. Thomas Merton was part of this history. Evelyn Waugh detected an ascetic dimension deep within American culture, which took form in unusual ways. Jacques Maritain declared that activism in America did not replace but merely masked a hunger for spiritual living and contemplation. To know America well, one must know something of the spiritual life.

Contemplation in America takes the form of fascination with the beyond and the nameless, with the indefinite future and the infinite possibility. Contemplation has something to do with allowing reality no limits. It also has something to do with seeing points of convergence where others, in despair, see only diversity. America has brought together in its history elements once seen as polarities rather than as points of connection: the government and the governed; the secular and the sacred; the requirements of authority and the right of dissent; capitalism and socialism; markets and entitlements; individuality and concern for the common effort.

Thomas Merton summed up an era. He showed us our spiritual potential in the midst of our secular endeavors. He made holiness equivalent with a life that seeks to be whole, honest, and free. He taught us that it was possible to be truly religious without being formally religious. He proved that contemplation could occur in the throes of restlessness and that it was permissible to be fully human.

Merton was part of the great Catholic tradition and yet seemed not to be confined by it. He saw in that tradition the capacity for a comprehensive synthesis of human thought, but he protested against institutional tendencies in the Catholic Church toward fascism. He observed that claims of infallibility and an insistence on mandatory celibacy would destroy its authority. He loved the liturgy and community life that Catholicism made possible, the spiritual tradition and sense of mysticism it encouraged, the humor and humanity that shone through its sometimes rigid structures. He was Catholic to the core because he would not allow Catholicism to particularize or parochialize him. He was against the Church "as established and worldly," against all in the Church that was "dirty" and "demonic." He defined fidelity as the capacity to condemn the lie in the Church, the refusal to canonize its sinfulness. But he saw also the beauty and splendor, the sincerity and love that the Catholic tradition could instill and inspire.

Merton was passionate about preserving his own individuality. In this, he is like Emerson, who declares in "Self-Reliance" that nothing is ultimately more sacred than the integrity of one's own spirit. In the last talk Merton delivered, on the day of his death, he defined alienation as the end result of a life lived according to conditions someone else determines. In *Contemplation in a World of Action*, he observed that alienation is an experience of the self kept as prisoner by another. A prisoner is locked into a system that allows no participation.

Merton spoke often of bondage in his prose and poetry. He protested against the slavery inflicted by the secular world on many and against the docility and obedience sometimes arbitrarily demanded by the Church. He would make his life a pawn in no system and yet would show, paradoxically, that he *belonged* to the world that could not own him and to the Church that could not possess him. In this, he reflected the era in which he lived and the culture in which he matured.

The appeal of the man is extraordinary. Much of it is tied up with his honesty. One might disagree with him, but one always knows that hypocrisy or pretension are not part of his life. From his honesty, a warm and vital humanity emerged. He had a capacity to speak to others as though they were speaking to themselves. The range of his writing, the extent of his following, are testimony of the universal, catholic comprehension of the man, of the cosmic Buddhist compassion with which he lived life. He let an entire century breathe through him because he inhaled it as the breath of his own life and was inspired by it. It was not the stale air of categories and systems, provincialisms and pettiness that he absorbed, but the oxygen of life that resists all boundaries, of truth that eludes all barriers, of love that evades all constraint.

There is sadness in the fact that he did not live longer. Yet, as he himself commented:

> We do not live more fully merely by doing more, seeing more, tasting more, and experiencing more…some of us need to discover that we will not begin to live more fully until we have the courage to do and see and taste and experience much less….[60]

The sadness we feel in his death may have something to do with the hope that he might have solved more of his problems or more of our problems had he lived longer. But we never solve our problems, he reminded us in his first major book, *The Seven Storey Mountain.* And so we accept each life on its own terms, each death in its own timing. Even in the dying there may be gain. The death in the East said something about Thomas Merton that further life in the West might have left unsaid.

In his brilliant book *Zen and the Birds of Appetite*, he quoted St. Ambrose to the effect that the return to paradise must be tested by fire. The avenging angel is posted at Eden with a flaming sword. As Ambrose interprets it, the flame forbids return but also signals the means by which return could occur. Paradise could be won again by fire—the fire of passion and the fire of love, the fire that destroys and cleanses all that is evil in us, the fire that renews and supports life by its light and its warmth.

Merton had been tested by fire. He had seen and said it all by the time death overcame him. There are always more opportunities and further possibilities. At some stage, however, the additional growth does not lead necessarily to larger meaning. The things Merton became at fifty years of age he had begun in his twenties. What he might have been at seventy, he indicated, for those who need to know this, in the many volumes of prose and poetry he authored.

There would always be something unfinished about Thomas Merton. It is that way with talented people. They are alive as long as they live.

They never fit into final categories.

John Eudes Bamberger, a fellow monk and friend of Merton, quoted a Haiku death poem in summing up Merton's elusiveness:

> Would you see to trace me?
> Ha! Try catching the tempest
> In a net.[61]

In a statement he made near the end of his life entitled "Day of a Stranger," he speaks of his unwillingness to respond in predictable ways to the two syllables that compose his last name. This statement is a prose poem in which he gives witness to some of the most personal experiences of his life.

"I can see no reason why a man can't love God and a woman at the same time," he observes. Nonetheless he feels an obligation to conserve "the stillness, the silence, the poverty, the virginal point of pure nothingness which is the center of all other loves."[62]

As a hermit, he is attuned to the rhythms of nature. He writes in a manner reminiscent of Thoreau:

> I receive from the eastern wood, the tall oaks, the one word "Day," which is never the same. It is never spoken in any known language.[63]

He has made of his day not only a reverent response to the timing of the universe but also a series of rituals that bind him to home and humankind:

> Rituals. Washing out the coffee pot in the rain bucket.... More rituals. Close all the windows on the south side (heat). Leave windows open on north and east sides (cool).... Pull down

> shades. Get water bottle. Rosary. Watch. Library book to be returned. It is time to visit the human race.[64]

Later:

> Soon I will cut bread, eat supper, say psalms, sit in the back room as the sun sets…[65]

The rituals included not only the tasks of the day but the trials of an era. He became part of what Dom Helder Camara called the "Abrahamic minority, i.e., that minority of men or women in every age of history who declare the meaning of the human when the majority is indifferent or hostile." He explains the reason for his elusiveness with people: "It is because I want to be more…than a friend, that I have become to all…a stranger."[66] He was judged by a famous Benedictine author in terms accorded few people:

> I am not giving in to an ingenious, admiring expression of friendship when I rank Merton with the Fathers of the Early Church and those of the Middle Ages.… His humanism explains why his message, as did theirs, has found so great an audience.[67]

For Flavian Burns, Merton's abbot and confessor, he can be compared to Bernard of Clairvaux, the quintessential Cistercian, one of the greatest saints and mystics in Christian history.

He wanted to understand all who suffer, as we have seen. This intention requires, of course, touching the entire human race. The touching depends, however, on undergoing the ordeal of fire, of sustaining creatively the pain that is the road back to paradise. It is the road of the cross that gives entrance to Eden and Easter. But it requires first the Gethsemane experience of blood and desertion, loneliness and heartbreak.

Merton was frank and candid. He raised questions that were rightly raised about whether we can declare totally who we are, at least to the degree we can comprehend this, and still be loved. Is it possible to be human openly? Can we let others see us thoroughly as we are, and hope to lead them, inspire them? Few took that risk with greater courage than Thomas Merton.

The risk was all the more difficult because he was essentially a shy man. In *The Inner Experience*, he describes the inner self as a shy wild animal that hides whenever a stranger is at hand and shows itself only when there is silence and the animal is alone. The description is apt not only for the inner self but for Thomas Merton himself.

The journey was long, but at the end there was neither weariness nor fatigue. There was neither bitterness nor even the memory of suffering sustained. He once described the end of history not as a time of settling accounts or closing books but as a final beginning, as a definitive birth. His life had gone that way. Every defeat was a new start; all the reverses were first steps; the many ways he died taught him the initial syllables for the next sentence.

The human journey is a circle. The universe does not go out forever in one direction but bends back on itself. The planet on which we live is a globe, so that all our pilgrimages are already homecomings. There is really no way out. No one is ever lost. We merely return by different paths. There is a paradox in that—one built into the fabric of the Gospel message: the goings forth are ways in which we remain near the ones we love. How the Zen Buddhists would appreciate that puzzle! Thomas Merton never left us. The journey continues.

ACKNOWLEDGMENTS

My life has centered around three vital institutions: the academic community, the ecclesial community, and domestic life. As I look back on the long endeavor required to publish this book, I am grateful for those who had a special role to play by their assistance. All of the people who come to mind are part of one of the three communities I have cited.

Ramapo College of New Jersey, the State's Public Liberal Arts College, where I serve as Distinguished Professor of Literature and Philosophy, provided me with a semester in which my teaching commitments were reduced by half. This, together with funding for research trips to Louisville, Kentucky, were indispensable to the completion of this book. In a particular way, I am grateful for the personal and professional assistance of Dr. John Robert Cassidy.

Fordham University in New York City, where I served as an adjunct professor of theology during the writing of the original edition of this book, is an institution that has a claim on my loyalties in many ways. I pursued a second doctorate there, in the field of English and American Literature. I am most conscious of the assistance and support of Drs. John Boyd, S.J., and Ewert Cousins in this regard.

Bellarmine University in Louisville presides over the Thomas Merton Studies Center, which contains the finest collection of Merton's published and unpublished material. I am grateful to the University administration, the faculty and a series of directors and archivists of the Thomas Merton Center who were unfailing in their kindness, professional competence, and personal availability. They received numerous letters, phone calls, and visits from me during the work on this book.

Louisville, Kentucky, is not only a city of cultural, historical, and academic worth; it is also a city associated with Thomas Merton and his circle of friends and associates. The three trustees of the Merton Legacy Trust granted permission to examine unpublished material, and generously made themselves available for interviews.

The second community that comes to mind as I reflect on assistance given to this project is the ecclesial community. The Abbey of Gethsemani, Trappist, Kentucky, offered me support, encouragement, and personal warmth. Brother Patrick Hart, Thomas Merton's secretary, is an exceptional man, someone who represents that rare blend of rich human and religious resources. I am also grateful for the interviews accorded me by Abbot James Fox and Abbot Flavian Burns. Both men followed for years an eremitical lifestyle. They agreed to see me, nonetheless, and dealt with my sometimes difficult questions with a candor and kindness that inspired me to want to do likewise.

Domestic life forms the final and most important community that supported me in this endeavor. This includes most particularly three remarkable women. My mother, Mary, helped to keep this book moving in ways that only mothers can. She nurtured my life personally and professionally to so great a degree that I am unthinkable without her. My sister, Rose Marie, gave me the support and admiration, the criticism, and dispassionate advice that only a younger sister can render. My wife, Theresa, has lived in all three communities I mentioned: academic, ecclesial, and domestic. Without her help, this book would simply not have been written. She taught me how ministry and marriage belong together. She helped me to learn how pure and faithful human love can be. In her heart, grace and beauty conspired to create an exceptional person.

Chapter One

1. Thomas Merton, *The Asian Journal of Thomas Merton,* (New York: New Directions, 1973), p. 152.
2. Thomas Merton, *My Argument with the Gestapo* (Garden City, N.Y.: Doubleday, 1969), p. 17.
3. Cf. Edward Rice, *The Man in the Sycamore Tree* (Garden City, N.Y.: Image, 1972), pp. 22–23. The author had interviews with friends of Merton who supported the fact but who chose not to be named as sources.
4. The romantic attachment Merton experienced to a nurse who attended him at the hospital in Louisville was confirmed by two of Merton's abbots, his secretary, a circle of friends in Louisville, and a close friend from his Columbia days. The author conducted interviews with all the people cited. The affair is addressed, with credible evidence, by Michael Mott, the official biographer of Merton. See Michael Mott, *The Seven Mountains of Thomas Merton* (Boston: Houghton Mifflin, 1984). Abundant documentation is present in Merton's poetry, published posthumously. See Thomas Merton, *Eighteen Poems* (New York: New Directions, 1985).
5. Interview of Merton's close friend, Edward Rice, with the author, May 20, 1979. The bar was Nick's at Seventh Avenue and West Tenth Street.
6. Merton, *My Argument with the Gestapo,* p. 51.
7. Thomas Merton, *A Vow of Conversation* (unpublished journals in Thomas Merton Studies Center, Bellarmine College, Louisville, Ky. June 26, 1965. Published many years later as *A Vow of Conversation* [New York: Farrar, Straus, Giroux, 1988], pp. 193–194).
8. Merton, *My Argument with the Gestapo,* p. 113.
9. Merton, *My Argument with the Gestapo,* p. 116.
10. Thomas Merton, *Exile Ends in Glory* (Milwaukee: Bruce, 1948), p. 142.

11. Thomas Merton, *Exile Ends in Glory*, p. 116.
12. Thomas Merton, *Seeds of Contemplation* (New York: New Directions, 1949), p. 87.
13. Merton, *The Asian Journal of Thomas Merton*, p. 236.

Chapter Two

14. Interview of the author with Abbot Flavian Burns, April 8, 1979.
15. Interview with Flavian Burns.
16. Interview of the author at the Abbey of Gethsemani with Abbot James Fox, April 8, 1979.
17. Interview with Flavian Burns.
18. Thomas Merton, *No Man Is an Island* (New York: Harcourt, Brace, 1955), p. 155.
19. Thomas Merton, *Seeds of Contemplation*, p. 44.
20. Thomas Merton, *Seeds of Contemplation,* p. 42.
21. Thomas Merton, *Seeds of Contemplation,* p. 65.
22. Thomas P. McDonnell, "An Interview with Thomas Merton," *Motive* 28 (1967), p. 41.
23. M. Basil Pennington, ed., *The Cistercian Spirit* (Spencer, Mass.: Cistercian, 1970), p. ix.
24. John Howard Griffin, *A Hidden Wholeness: The Visual World of Thomas Merton* (Boston: Houghton Mifflin, 1970), p. 1.
25. Thomas Merton and Robert Lax, *A Catch of Anti-Letters* (Kansas City: Sheed, Andrews and McMeel, 1978), p. 24.
26. Thomas Merton, "First and Last Thoughts: An Author's Preface," in Thomas P. McDonnell, *A Thomas Merton Reader*, rev. ed. (Garden City, N.Y.: Image, 1974), p. 17.
27. Thomas Merton, *Eighteen Poems* (New York: New Directions, 1985).
28. Maxwell Geismer, as quoted in the *John Howard Griffin Reader*, ed. Daniel Bradford (Boston: Houghton Mifflin, 1968), p. 21.

Chapter Three

29. Thomas Merton, *The Behavior of Titans* (New York: New Directions, 1961), p. 7.
30. Thomas Merton, *Mystics and Zen Masters* (New York: Farrar, Straus and Giroux, 1967), p. 212.
31. Thomas Merton, *Conjectures of a Guilty Bystander* (Garden City, N.Y.: Image, 1968), pp. 156–157.

32. Thomas Merton, *Conjectures of a Guilty Bystander,* p. 21.
33. Thomas Merton, *Opening the Bible* (Collegeville, Minn.: Liturgical, 1970), p. 27.
34. Thomas Merton, *Opening the Bible,* p. 70.
35. Thomas Merton, *Faith and Violence* (Notre Dame, Ind.: University of Notre Dame Press, 1968), p. 8.
36. Thomas Merton, *Clement of Alexandria* (New York: New Directions, 1962), p. 13.
37. Thomas Merton, *Conjectures of a Guilty Bystander,* p. 285.

Chapter Four

38. Thomas Merton, *Thoughts in Solitude* (New York: Farrar, Straus and Cudahy, 1958), p. 91.
39. Thomas Merton, *Life and Holiness* (Garden City, N.Y.: Image, 1964), p. 25.
40. Thomas Merton, *The Ascent to Truth* (New York: Harcourt, Brace, 1951), p. 300.
41. Thomas Merton, *Seeds of Contemplation,* p. 169.

Chapter Five

42. Thomas Merton, *The Seven Storey Mountain* (New York: Harcourt, Brace, 1948), p. 23.
43. Merton, *The Seven Storey Mountain,* pp. 398–399.
44. Thomas Merton, *Boris Pasternak/Thomas Merton: Six Letters* (Lexington, Ky.: The King Library Press, University of Kentucky, 1973), p. 11.
45. Thomas Merton, *Cables to the Ace* (New York: New Directions, 1968), pp. 55–56.
46. Thomas Merton, *Cables to the Ace,* p. 206.
47. Thomas Merton, *Cables to the Ace,* Sec. 51.
48. Thomas Merton, *Cables to the Ace,* Sec 60.
49. Thomas Merton, *The Sign of Jonas* (New York: Harcourt, Brace, 1953), pp. 90–91.
50. Thomas Merton, ed., *Gandhi on Non-Violence* (New York: New Directions, 1965), p. 64.

Chapter Six

51. Thomas Merton, *Original Child Bomb* (New York: New Directions, 1962), p. 18.
52. Thomas Merton, *Seeds of Contemplation,* p. 24.

53. Thomas Merton, *Collected Essays: Christian Humanism* (Louisville: Thomas Merton Studies Center), Vol. 6, pp. 164–222.
54. Thomas Merton, *The Collected Poems of Thomas Merton* (New York: New Directions, 1977).
55. Interview with James Fox.
56. Thomas Merton, *Mystics and Zen Masters* (New York: Farrar, Straus and Giroux, 1967), pp. 59–63.
57. Thomas Merton, *The Geography of Lograire* (New York: New Directions, 1969), North, I, 3.
58. Hari Prasad Shastri, trans., *Ashtavakra Gita* (London: Shanit Sadan, 1984).
59. I am grateful to Gail Ramshaw Schmidt and her doctoral dissertation, *The Poetry of Thomas Merton* (Madison, Wisc.: University of Wisconsin, 1976), for many fine insights into *Cables to the Ace* and *The Geography of Lograire.*

CHAPTER SEVEN

60. Thomas Merton, *No Man Is an Island* (New York: Harcourt, Brace, 1955), p. 122.
61. Patrick Hart, ed., *Thomas Merton: Monk* (Garden City, N.Y.: Image, 1976), p. 45.
62. Thomas P. McDonnell, ed., *A Thomas Merton Reader* (Garden City, N.Y.: Image, 1974), p. 434.
63. McDonnell, p. 435.
64. McDonnell, p. 435.
65. McDonnell, p. 437.
66. Thomas Merton, Japanese Edition: "Introduction to the Seven Storey Mountain" ("The Queen's Work," v. 56 N.T., 1964), p. 10.
67. Jean Leclerq, "Introduction, Contemplation in a World of Action" (Garden City, N.Y.: Image, 1973), p. 18.